BE A GREAT BOSS

ONE YEAR TO SUCCESS

ALA GUIDES FOR THE BUSY LIBRARIAN

HIRING, TRAINING, AND SUPERVISING LIBRARY SHELVERS
by Patricia Tunstall

WRITING AND PUBLISHING: THE LIBRARIAN'S HANDBOOK
edited by Carol Smallwood

MENTORING AT THE LIBRARY
by Marta K. Lee

MANAGING LIBRARY VOLUNTEERS: A PRACTICAL TOOLKIT, SECOND EDITION
by Preston Driggers and Eileen Dumas

WHAT THEY DON'T TEACH YOU IN LIBRARY SCHOOL
by Elisabeth Doucett

BE A GREAT BOSS

ONE YEAR TO SUCCESS

CATHERINE HAKALA-AUSPERK

AMERICAN LIBRARY ASSOCIATION
CHICAGO 2011

Catherine Hakala-Ausperk is the deputy director of the Cleveland Heights–University Heights (Ohio) Public Library. A frequent speaker at national and state conferences, staff days, and workshops, she has a passion for supporting, coaching, and developing successful library staff, including bosses. A twenty-five-year public library veteran, she is also an adjunct faculty member of Kent State University's School of Library and Information Science and has been a guest editor and author for ALA/APA's *Library Worklife.* Hakala-Ausperk is a Certified Public Library Administrator (CPLA).

ALA Editions purchases fund advocacy, awareness, and accreditation programs for library professionals worldwide.

ISBN-13: 978-0-8389-1068-9

Printed in the United States of America
15 14 13 12 11 5 4 3 2 1

Library of Congress Cataloging-in-Publication Data
Hakala-Ausperk, Catherine.
Be a great boss : one year to success / Catherine Hakala-Ausperk.
p. cm. -- (ALA guides for the busy librarian)
Includes bibliographical references and index.
ISBN 978-0-8389-1068-9 (alk. paper)
1. Library personnel management--Handbooks, manuals, etc. 2. Supervision of employees--Handbooks, manuals, etc. 3. Library administration--Handbooks, manuals, etc. I. Title.
Z682.H16 2011
023'.9--dc22
2010014047

Book design in Charis SIL and Interstate by Casey Bayer.

♾ This paper meets the requirements of ANSI/NISO Z39.48-1992 (Permanence of Paper).

ALA Editions also publishes its books in a variety of electronic formats. For more information, visit the ALA Store at www.alastore.ala.org and select eEditions.

CONTENTS

PREFACE

You've just been promoted, or maybe you've just appointed a new person to be the "boss." Maybe you or they are the new page supervisor, or perhaps the technical services director, or, who knows, it could be the director.

You know just what it takes to succeed. A new boss needs to attend a couple dozen workshops, take a few classes, read a few of the right books, and hook up with some excellent role models or coaches and find a mentor.

But who has the time—or money—for that? Success needs to come a lot faster.

This workbook can help.

Not only will it cover, in just one year, key issues and realities that all bosses need to know but also, and perhaps more important, it will introduce and establish a development and learning style that will perpetuate year after year.

Nobody wants to fail. Every boss really *wants* to be a "great" boss.

In order to make that happen, there's a lot of work to do . . .

PREFACE

ACKNOWLEDGMENTS

I've been blessed thus far in my career with too many people to thank. And I'm not done yet! This is a great problem to have, and appreciating it is what led me to want to write this book in the first place. I will be forever indebted to all of them for the support and encouragement they offered me.

At work, there's been Jane, Marguerite, Vivian, Jim, Cathy, Holly, Steve, Kim, and, of course, JoAnn D.

But my most ardent supporters have always been my husband, Dale, and my sister, Susan.

Thanks to all of you.

INTRODUCTION

This is not a textbook.

There are plenty of them out there, if that's what you're looking for. Richard Rubin, a mentor and my first library school professor, wrote the classic *Human Resources Management in Libraries: Theory and Practice.* You could read that if you're looking for a classic, traditional textbook. Actually, I credit this disclaimer to Rubin, who is also Kent State University's library school dean, because he once opened a human resources lecture I attended by saying, "I am not a lawyer. I am not a lawyer. I am not a lawyer."

Well, this is not a textbook.

What this *is* is a workbook . . . and you're going to do the work. Within these pages is a compilation of trusted, experienced, and knowledgeable advice in areas you'll need to master in order to be a better boss. If you have people around to help you develop your skills, you're as lucky as I've been. But the more I travel around the country and talk to library leaders who are floundering, the more I've come to realize that not everyone is that lucky.

And here's one more thing that this book is *not.* It's not just one person's (my) opinion of what makes a person a good boss. Over the past twenty-five years I've collected, written, spoken, presented, whispered, conferenced, published, and otherwise handed down advice from some leading experts on libraries, management, leadership, and (now, don't roll your eyes if this sounds corny) life. It's all here.

And what do you have to contribute to attain success? Just one hour a week.

That's it. But, simple as that sounds, it's nonnegotiable. And, hey, I'm really doing you a big favor. If you haven't heard by now, managers, leaders, bosses *never* plan time in their schedules to just stop working and think. And we need to. All of us. So by the time you finish this workbook, you're not only going to be a great (or better) boss, you will have also developed the phenomenally productive habit of setting at least one hour aside every single week to think, reflect, and plan and, as a result, you're going to continue getting better all the time.

How does it work? It's easy. Start by getting out your calendar, whether you write it down, memorize it (oh, those were the days), store it online, or chip it in stone. The first thing you *have* to do is block off one hour a week to work through this book. Every month's topic, every week's readings, even your homework exercises are going to help you develop the skills you really need in your job. So frame out a schedule to get through this workbook, get it down, get it in writing, get it in place, even if you have to move some sessions around because something comes up. A piece of advice: don't try to read through the whole book at once. It won't be as much fun, you won't really do the thoughtful work you need to do, and, well, it just isn't that easy.

Give yourself time to learn. There's a lot you have to think about. If being a great boss was just pushing papers around, anyone could do it. Give yourself this year and then, when you feel better about yourself, you can start helping someone else.

In the end, we all win as our libraries improve.

In these pages, week by week, you'll be asked to consider just about every aspect of a boss's job. You'll just think about some, you'll read about others, and then you'll apply it all in the exercises that follow each section.

Wait a minute. Don't even *try* to argue that you don't have the time for this process. Most of us, probably all of us, *waste* at least one hour each week doing something we don't need to do, redoing something someone else already did, or just cutting a day short here or there. If you absolutely, positively can't find this time, then give up a lunch hour or come in early once a week. Or, if you must, work at home, on your own time.

You'll grow. You'll come to feel that all the authors and speakers and teachers within these pages are friends of yours, just like mentors with offices right down the hall. All of their shared wisdom and valuable advice will come back to you right when you need it and, best of all, your staff—and your customers—will see you become a stronger, more effective, and happier boss.

Write in this book as you go. (I know that's not easy for librarians, but really, it's okay.) Tuck copies of articles in the pages. Send excerpts to friends and to new bosses or those who could use a refresher. Share what you're learning with your colleagues. Have fun.

Someone someday will be talking about the time they spent working for you. Maybe they'll be counseling someone who is thinking of applying for your staff. "Don't worry about the drive or the pay or even the job," they'll confide, "just take it! It's worth it just to work for such a great boss!"

Attitude

WEEK ONE | THE ATTITUDE YOU DISPLAY

If you aren't going to read this chapter, then don't bother with this book.

The title of this chapter is no joke. Your attitude is everything. With the right attitude, you can become a great boss. People will *want* to work for you. Staff will turn down better job offers if it means leaving your library. Your successes will be legendary. With the wrong attitude, you're going to count the days to retirement, like a ten-year-old waiting for summer vacation. Think about it.

This is the most important choice you'll make, and it will determine every aspect of your success from this point on.

I hope you are a boss for the right reasons. That is, I hope you have become a boss because you wanted to be one, not because you were the last person left standing, so to speak. Or, worse yet, not because you were the best at doing the tasks that were required of your old job. It's happened. I'm sure you've seen it too. The very best librarian, the "reference queen," gets moved into the branch manager's job when it opens up. She has had absolutely no managerial or supervisory training. She's never, in all her years, shown even the most marginal interest in supervising others or offering "big picture" ideas. So now she's the boss and all the boss stuff is sitting, undone, on her desk. But she's still out there on the floor, answering the complex questions in record time. Great. That's just great. But who's running the show?

I urge you to take some time today to think about the power that your supervisor's attitude has always had over your life—both at work and beyond. Early in my career, before online schedules, we were allowed to make copies of the printed schedules and take them home. Mine hung on my refrigerator. After getting three kids ready for school, packing five lunches, and (usually) cleaning up after the dog, I was ready to race out the door to work. But first I'd stop at the refrigerator to see who my "boss" or the PIC (person in charge) would be that day. On that point, the rest of my day hung in the balance. I'd see that it was either "Yeah, fun, whew. This should be a good day" or "Damn. It's Captain Moody today. This is going to be a looooong one."

Does your staff need that? Hardly. Remember the kids and the lunches and the life I mentioned earlier? I believe that every single employee has the right to have a good boss. One that is in the job for the right reasons. One whose attitude reflects positivity, respect, support, and encouragement. None of us needs to spend our days ducking away from emotional, moody, unresponsive, and unsupportive supervisors. We have enough to deal with in our "real" lives. How can we ever expect our employees to have the right attitude if their bosses don't?

If things like hissy fits, moodiness, playing favorites, and so on describe you, then you need this book but it probably won't do any good. Unless you're ready to change your attitude.

When you become the boss, please realize that you literally hold the lives and, in large part, the happiness of all of your staff members in your hands. Schedules, budgets, furniture selection, and Chamber of Commerce luncheons aside, the single most inarguably important part of the attitude you display must be this: *Treat your staff well.* It is within your power. You *can* do it. How?

Attitude is your paintbrush. It colors every situation.[1]

Adjust your attitude.

Here's one of the best frames of reference about attitude that I've ever heard. It's called "Permanent Whitewater" and I give full credit for it to John Schreiber and Becky Shannon, who for years facilitated Ohio's Library Leadership Institute. I share this with all the new bosses I have the privilege to train.

Whether you are going to be the boss for one day a month or every single day from today on, you need to come to the library each morning expecting *permanent whitewater*. Expecting chaos. Expecting the need to make decisions, solve problems, and provide stable direction and leadership. When you close the car door in the morning and walk toward your library, you should not be thinking "I hope I can finish that annual report draft before lunch, so I can get caught up on those late evaluations. And I've got to get those schedules done and the budget started. Nobody better try to interrupt me."

Instead, put on a life vest and wade in with the *right* attitude: "Okay, I'm not going to get to that annual report draft today. I better be sure to walk around the building to see if I can help keep things to a dull roar. *We* might have a couple of people call in sick; something's been going around. I'll make some changes to the schedule. Hmmm, I wonder how Dave's mother is doing in the hospital."

Being prepared for permanent whitewater will give you the attitude you need for that day, and then you can expand that to fill the whole year, as well as the next. You'll still get your work done. But you'll be putting the people whose lives you touch first.

Now, that's a great boss!

The KEYS to PERMANENT WHITEWATER

- Keep paddling
- Cooperate from front to back
- Steer!
- Pull over every once in a while and rest
- Dodge all the rocks you can
- Be prepared to flip—and right yourself again
- Switch sides once in a while
- Wear life jackets
- Lock yourself in for the bad parts
- Know you'll get wet[2]

WORKSHEET

Welcome to your first homework exercise. Don't skip it. A big part of the development process you're in for the year will include your participation in these journaling, researching, and reflective exercises. So go ahead. Your hour isn't up yet.

1. **Think back to** the worst boss you've ever had (no names, please). How would you describe her or his attitude?

2. **Think of an** example of something you saw a boss do to you or a coworker that had a significant, negative impact on them. What was it, and how could the *right* attitude have made a difference?

3. **How about your** best boss ever; how was her or his attitude different? How could you tell?

4. **Search for some** articles (you notice I didn't say "Google some articles"; I assume you have excellent database access as well). Read at least three with suggestions on getting and keeping the right attitude for leadership. Print them out, if you like, and clip them to this page. Summarize them here. What did you learn?

5. **Hopefully, you've got** a little bit of your hour left. Now, please go do something. Nothing to write down for that. It's time to get out of your office and practice a little "MBWA" ("Management by Walking Around"). Go observe the attitude your staff members exhibit and those of other supervisors, if there are any. If you find some bad examples, start thinking of ways to offer coaching for improvement. Say something exceptionally nice to the first employee you see when you step away from this book. Or just pitch in at the circulation desk and help out. Or pick something else. Do *anything* that shows the attitude of a great boss!

Attitude

WEEK TWO | HOW TO TREAT OTHERS

There was once a boss who presented a personnel evaluation to a subordinate while riding in an elevator. In a two-story library. No kidding. This chapter (and welcome back, by the way) isn't about brain surgery. It's about how to treat others. When you're the boss, that matters a lot more than it used to. If attitude is the most important characteristic of a good boss (and it is), then how you apply that attitude and how you show it in your treatment of others is a close second.

We've all seen and heard of the bad examples, right? Yelling at someone during a meeting, in front of peers. Spreading gossip about employees or other confidential matters to peers, only to have it get back to the employee eventually. (We're in the information business, right? Gossip in libraries has about the same shelf life as ice cream on the beach.) I've known bosses who wouldn't even return a simple "Hello" in the hallway or who would throw a staff member under the bus—rather than take responsibility themselves—faster than you can say "bad morale."

Here's a story that's almost unbelievable, yet it's true. It, for me, is the ultimate example of how *not* to treat another human being. A single mom was very proud of her son, who had just graduated from a military academy and was being shipped overseas for two years. She was pleased to have been scheduled for the early shift on the day of his departure, so she knew she could get him to the airport in plenty of time. But as that day drew near and she thought more about how long it would be before she'd see him again, she realized she needed more time. Reluctantly, sheepishly, apologetically (none of which should have applied), she called her boss and asked for the whole day off as personal time.

"I can't keep messing with the schedule every time someone comes up with something new," was her boss's reply. It gets worse. "Not only that," she continued, "if I let you do that this time, you're going to want to take time off every single time he gets deployed!"

Not brain surgery here, right? We come to work every day. Statistics have well documented the fact that we spend more time at work than at home, with our families. So how should we treat those with whom we spend all this time when we're the boss? You know or you wouldn't be investing your time in this development program. Of course you know how valuable your staff are. What you might not know is how important you are to them and how your treatment of them can affect absolutely everything.

Don't tell me you get too busy or too stressed to remember this. That's part of what this one-hour-per-week time is for. Think every day, every week, and every year about how you treat others. It gets easier and, on this foundation, you can build every single other strength you'll need to become a great boss.

Without this foundation, though, you—and they—are in trouble.

How we spend our days is how we spend our lives.[3]

With whom will you interact this week? Are they new, frightened, and overwhelmed? How can you help? What would you want to happen, if you were in their position? Sure, your budget is due at the end of the month, but didn't that librarian who just walked by look a little troubled? Do you wonder what she was doing hovering around your door? Maybe she needs help?

Every single interaction you have (yep, you don't get bad days as the boss; stay home if you can't be kind and respectful, and try it again tomorrow) will build or destroy the very basis of your relationships with your staff. You're going to ask a lot of them and you know it. If you've remembered the keys: respect, honesty, integrity, consistency, humor, flexibility . . . you're going to have an army on your side. If you ignore these gifts and treat your staff badly, I hope you know how to do everything because you're going to be literally and figuratively on your own.

And what of your reward? Are you in this for the money? If so, poor thing, you're probably going to be disappointed. But you're not, I'm sure. Library staffs are made up of the most dedicated, creative, professional people most of us have ever known, and when you get to be the boss, whether by accident or design, you're in it to make a difference and you can.

One more story. The librarian calls in and gets his manager on the phone early one morning. His mother has had a stroke and he needs to jump on a plane and get to her. He begins telling her where his book discussion materials are, which customers are waiting for the DVDs he's been processing and . . . she stops him. "Don't worry about us," she tells him. "Right now, your family is the most important thing. We'll figure things out here. Just go and take care and we'll be thinking of you." She didn't have any ulterior motive for saying that. She wasn't trying to cheaply and ineffectually condescend to him. She meant it and you'd mean it too, and as a result, she has created a loyal, appreciative staff member for life.

That's how you treat people when you're a really *great* boss.

WORKSHEET

Last week, you reflected on your attitude. What we all need to remember is that while having the right attitude is important, *showing* it is paramount. So let's spend the rest of this week's time thinking about how you demonstrate your attitude by how you treat your employees.

1. **Do you have** a folder for each and every person you supervise? You should. And into that folder you should be putting all notes formal and informal that you're going to use during required evaluations and, more serendipitously, when you just want to encourage them. If you don't already have these folders made, make them now. Then think about each person individually and put a note in their file (and on your calendar) listing one thing you can do to show them kindness and respect in the coming week.

2. **What's the worst** treatment you've ever seen a staff member get from their supervisor? This could be something that happened to you or to someone else. Use ten words to describe how it was damaging to that person. How else could the situation have been handled? Write a scenario that would have been better and explain why.

3. **Imagine you've been** asked to speak to a library school class on management. Here's the first question the students pose to you. "If it's so hard to be the boss, juggling all the responsibilities and deadlines and pressures and people's problems, then why is it worth it? Why not let somebody else handle all the staffing headaches?" How would you answer that?

4. **You have a** boss now, right? Even if you're the director, you have a board of directors. List ten different ways your boss could treat you better.

5. **If all of** those things actually happened, what changes would it make for you?

Here's the part where you put this workbook away for a while and get out of your office with your remaining time. Just like last week, go walk around. I'll bet you can find at least one or two opportunities to treat one of your staff members well.

Attitude

WEEK THREE | INSTILL CONFIDENCE

"When in danger or in doubt, run in circles, scream and shout."

Yep, it's true. Staff really do make up stuff like that about their bosses. This was a popular refrain in one library where the manager could be counted on for little else but disappointment. Does that describe you?

Remember, this project is all about "development," and in order to grow, we all have to face our own weaknesses as bosses and commit to make changes for the better. So, what is it about you that inspires confidence?

Maybe the clearest way to look at this is to think about places where you *don't* want to work. Why do people avoid applying there? I'd be willing to bet that a lot of your trepidation has to do with the strengths, or lack thereof, of that particular library's leaders. Let's face it: we're all more comfortable when the buck is stopping on the desk of someone who can handle it.

In my many library positions, I've enjoyed my work the most, inarguably, when I admired and learned from my boss. When I had all confidence that she could handle her job and still look forward to new successes for the library and for me. With bosses like that, you knew where they stood. Agree with them or not, you knew where they were taking the organization and down which paths you would not be going.

One of my supervisors used to say, "No mistake is final." That was oddly comforting. Our confidence was maintained that we would always rise above problems and find solutions, even though we clearly knew that we'd all be making mistakes along the way. We were confident, though, that the boss would lead us forward. That same person used to also say (often to students in management classes, studying to become bosses), "When you're faced with a challenging decision, whatever you do, make a damn decision! Whether you end up being right or wrong . . . *Make a decision!*"

And he was right. Decision-making is a confidence builder and, over time, helps inspire in your staff a sense of trust that you'll keep them on track, one way or another. That person inspired confidence, and that's important in a boss. How can you do that?

First of all, make sure your staff know what you stand for. Be clear. Be repetitive. Be focused. Don't change your mind every time you speak or listen to someone with a different opinion. Have a vision and stick to it and your staff will come to understand that they can trust you to be strong. And by the way, *strong* isn't a bad word. I remember back in the 1970s, during the Women's Movement, there was an ongoing debate about the difference between being *aggressive* and *assertive*. Turns out, they're not synonymous. Assertive leaders show confidence and strength. And neither is a four-letter word, especially for a great boss.

In order to build that confidence in your staff, both they and you need to know what you really stand for and they need to be able to explain it in a short elevator ride. Succinct. Focused. To the point. Strong. These are all characteristics of a leader who can be trusted. So what is it for you? Is it customer service above all else? Or is it literacy for everyone in your community? Are you bound and determined to work hand in hand with your schools, or are decorum and civility your goal?

Pick one. Believe in it and be consistent in your decision-making in support of it. But don't stop there. Don't keep your (and, as the boss, it's now your library's) focus your little secret. Let your staff hear you talk about it. Let your staff see you work toward it. Let your community hear you speak, read your columns, and meet you in the library, talking about what you're all about. Visit staff meetings. Write a blog. Put a letter in a bottle. Give everyone you supervise confidence that they're on the right bus, in the right class, on the right team to move them forward each and every day.

When my library made the decision to become a proactive reference, customer-focused institution, it was our library director who steered the ship from day one. Some staff members were tentatively on board, others were on the fence, and a few were climbing over it, trying to get away. We were remodeling our main library, and in it there would be no reference desks and no circulation desk. A big step, but one that many of us, including our boss, were convinced was the only path to the successful future of libraries. But first he needed to build confidence in that pathway. So he started by writing a philosophy statement, on the basis of which dozens of practical operational decisions would be made. He called this new approach "Quality Information Service." Here's how he started building confidence in this major change, which has since become the bedrock of our very innovative and successful library:

> I stopped using [a large department store] a number of years ago. My decision had nothing to do with the quality of their merchandise. Rather, it was [the store's] decision to both reduce the number of sales clerks and to consolidate them at "centralized" points within the store. Although I could generally spot a sales person because they were the ones wearing dresses or ties, they never seemed to be where I needed them to be. I had to go to one of those central points

CONFIDENCE-BUILDING SKILLS THAT MATTER

Employees want bosses who are both intellectually *and* emotionally intelligent. Does this describe you? If not, you have a goal.

Be Self-Aware and Socially Aware

- Recognize your own emotions
- Know your strengths and weaknesses
- Be certain about your capabilities and worth
- Be compassionate
- Recognize the feelings of others
- Anticipate and meet needs

Manage Yourself and the Relationships around You

- Isolate your disruptive impulses and control them
- Be honest
- Demonstrate integrity
- Take responsibility
- Be flexible
- Handle change well
- Be ready to act
- Sense what others need for growth
- Be persuasive
- Negotiate
- Resolve
- Nurture growth everywhere
- Create synergy[4]

to see if someone was free to return with me to the shelves. They aren't the only game in town so I now shop where the quality is as high but the service is better *and* easier to find. . . . What does this have to do with providing information in a public library today? Absolutely everything. The public service managers have worked together to develop the attached statement about "Providing Quality Information Service." It describes what we see as our future as we respond to requests for information throughout our system. Hopefully, it also explains the reasoning for several changes we've already made. We are ready now to bring it to you for your input since it falls on you to implement the concepts and practices described here.[5]

This document, as well as the many meetings, lectures, and conversations that followed it, established confidence in our boss during a time of significant transition.

No matter what you do as a boss from today forward, be confident that it's the right thing for the moment, then share your feelings, your gut, your commitment with your staff, so they can be confident too. That's an important building block for a good or great manager. And it will continue to pay benefits through all else you will do.

After all, remember, no mistake is final.

WORKSHEET

3

1. **What's the one** library boss you know or have heard of for whom you would never want to work? Why?

2. **If you could** "design" your perfect boss, what characteristics would she have?

3. **Why is it** important to have confidence in someone for whom you work? Does it really matter?

4. **If, on a** one-floor elevator ride, one of your most long-term employees was asked, "So, what's your boss really all about?" how would she respond?

5. **What one thing** about yourself would you most like to change, so that your staff could have *more* confidence in you? How can you start to bring about that change?

Attitude

WEEK FOUR | LEAD, MODEL, AND MOTIVATE

I've heard many managers complain over the years about how much they dislike hearing that "staff morale is low." It seems, they contend, like fighting a losing battle. To some extent, I agree. "We're not running an amusement park here," one of my more cynical peers once commented. She asked, "Since when did it become a necessity to provide your staff with a job, a salary, benefits . . . *and happiness*?"

Fair enough. To a point. But as bosses, we have made a commitment to provide aspects of the job that can end up equating to high morale . . . I would argue that the final outcome is then up to the employee.

So what are those components? I think effective bosses need to lead, model, and motivate. That's more than a salary but less than utopia. If you're good at it, though, and, more important, if you really feel it and mean it, you're going to find morale high at your library and service levels will be on the rise.

If you remember last week's section on building confidence and the example I gave of one director's introduction to what he called "Quality Information Service," you'll see leadership in action. What was the backbone of that leadership? It started with more than one person. A true leader builds consensus, for one thing. The library that proceeded with the development of proactive service was doing it based on a newly adopted system of philosophy but was also acting with the advice, support, and encouragement of the entire administrative team. The moral of this is: *don't lead alone.*

And why should you? If your vision is clear and you get your key staff behind you, then *leadership* at your library won't just refer to one person but to a stronger, more cohesive team whose diversity, creativity, and dedication can keep making forward progress.

I've had a lot of role models in my career, but my best (and favorite) one just never stops working. Whether in her library system or outside of it, she can be found teaching, coaching, speaking, planning, and generally motivating library staff all over northeast Ohio. She's my *model.* Mahatma Gandhi said: "Be the change you want to see in the world." That sounds a lot like "Be the model you want to have at work" to me. Have you been approached yet to go and speak to a library school class or at a nearby system's staff development day? If you have, then I hope you've accepted. If you haven't done so yet, it looks like it's time to volunteer.

There can be no real measure of the value of role modeling to your staff, to your peers, and to your superiors. Hundreds of business books can describe it in many different ways, but it's really simple, isn't it? It's a "put your money where your mouth is" situation. Bosses can have an expectation of how their staff should behave and be productive and show initiative, but if they don't show the same themselves, then it's really all just rhetoric. Model the library staff you want and let them see the value in following your lead. You'll fine-tune this over the years, but don't be afraid you're not good enough to get started right. It's not hard. Choose some really, really simple examples, making sure they come from the heart.

Now we're back to "I never promised you a rose garden." Motivating is seen by many bosses as frivolous, at best. You give your staff a job, right? You pay them, right? So why should you have to go further to "motivate" them to work for you? At a wonderful workshop back in the 1990s, the speaker instructed us to number a piece of paper from 1 to 10, and then to list 10 reasons why we work. We did so. The first 5 or 6 are pretty easy. After that, you're really thinking.

Next (and we didn't know there would be more), she asked us to number the back of the page from 1 to 10 and list 10 reasons why we work *hard.* Those reasons were our true motivations. They got to feelings we had deep inside us, to values and things that mattered even more than a paycheck. Do you have to buy donuts every morning to motivate your staff? Hardly. But you do need to find a way to get down into those last 10 reasons, find out what they are, and support them.

Bosses who do that effectively are the ones whose libraries matter.

The PERFECT MODEL

- Share everything
- Play fair
- Don't hit people
- Put things back where you found them
- Clean up your own mess
- Don't take things that aren't yours
- Say you're sorry when you hurt somebody
- Wash your hands before you eat
- Flush
- Warm cookies and milk are good for you
- Live a balanced life
- Take a nap every afternoon
- When you go out into the world . . . stick together
- Wonder

Take any one of those items and extrapolate it into sophisticated adult terms and apply it to your family life or your work . . . and it holds true and clear and firm.[6]

Suggested Reading

Fulghum, Robert. *All I Really Need to Know I Learned in Kindergarten.* New York: Ballantine Books, 2004.

WORKSHEET

1. **Who is your** hero? Why? Think about and list the characteristics of the three people whom you consider to be life or professional (or both) role models.

2. **Complete this sentence:** "Of all the bosses I've ever had, in any job, I think I'm the most like ___________ because of the way I ___________."

3. **Now finish this** one: "Of all the bosses I've ever had, in any job, I would like to be *more* like ___________, because ___________."

4. **You knew this** was coming . . . List ten reasons why you work.

5. **Now, list ten** reasons why you work *hard*. This will be what really motivates you!

6. **Ask a group** of your staff, including your managers and line staff, to describe in one sentence what your library philosophy is. What is it that you (and your library) stand for? Consider the results. Is your leadership clear enough?

Success with Stakeholders

WEEK ONE | YOUR BOARD

Let's just say it out loud and admit that, first and foremost, anyone who would volunteer their time, often in an industry whose operations are totally foreign to them, and who would eagerly attend night meetings, day meetings, trainings, seminars, and other outings for the benefit of their libraries deserves our utmost respect and appreciation.

But let's be honest too. There are as many horror stories out there about "Boards from Hell" as there are titles by Danielle Steel. So whether you're the department boss or the branch manager or the director . . . how do you deal with your board?

First and foremost, you deal with them patiently.

To say new board members have a lot to learn about libraries is true, and yet this really only speaks to one of the smallest of the hurdles they and you face. What's bigger? They have to learn to be board members. And that's an even tougher tightrope walk.

First, most feel they were selected or appointed or elected because of a particular strength or experience they bring, and that's probably partly true. But while they sit at your meetings and make decisions about your future, they have to wear another hat too, and that's the harder one to grasp for most. The second "role" they play is that of "Joe Community." They each are expected to represent the overall community they serve and see to it that the library's policy stays on track with community-relevant interests.

That's where you come in. You must *patiently* remind them to stay focused on the policy end of your operation and let you or your director do the administrating.

Next, you should deal with your board respectfully. Help them learn. Acknowledge that it's *their* town and *their* neighbors being represented. Even if you live nearby too, you still have a more personal interest in the job. So while you're being clear and firm about where their role stops and yours begins, be respectful and understand that they'll need some time to catch on.

And finally, deal with your board *consistently*. Set a high standard from the beginning for how quickly you'll answer their e-mails and calls, how thoroughly you'll prepare the massive amounts of paperwork they'll be perusing, and how simply and comprehensively you'll be presenting issues for their consideration, with all sides of an issue or problem represented. Once the board trusts you to be outstanding at *your* job, they can spend more time learning how to become better at theirs. Until then, they're going to be spinning everyone's wheels trying to do both.

One last suggestion is to be sure your staff know the board and vice versa. Rotate assignments for attending board meetings. Have staff make short (very short, because everyone's tired at 8:30 at night) presentations at the end of each board meeting to share or demonstrate something about the library's services that might be new. Actually, for your new board members, everything is new. Put their pictures and names up in your buildings, so both staff and customers can recognize them, literally and figuratively, for all they do.

What should you do if you're still having problems with your board? The same thing you should do with *all* your problems . . . ask your more experienced colleagues for help and advice. We're all in this together, and when we put our heads together, we've seen it all.

WHY ARE THEY HERE?

Why would a person seek or accept a job in the public domain that sometimes draws criticism, pays nothing, is time-consuming, requires great diplomacy, and deals with a never-ending stream of complex problems, the solutions to which are often hard-won compromises?

- Because they believe strongly in the importance of libraries to their community
- Because they feel the need to represent the interests of the community to the library director and to the funding agencies
- To try to preserve what they see as traditional library service in light of the overwhelming influence of technology
- Because many see a responsibility to oversee the fair and ethical expenditure of public tax dollars
- Because of the social prestige[1]

WORKSHEET

1. **How well do** you know your board members? Whether you're in a school or public library or even with a special organization, you can't possibly know them well enough. They're too important, especially to the bosses. Compile a brief biography of each member and attach it to this workbook. Include as much info as you can find about them. And while you're at it, share your final document with the rest of the staff and, if possible, with your customers, so they can all get to know the board better too.

2. **Find an online** board orientation training program and review it. Or review your library's, if you're lucky enough to have one. There are some great examples on WebJunction and also on the websites of many state library organizations. What do they focus on? What do people need to learn about libraries in order to become good trustees? Once you've answered that question, jot some notes about how you can help better prepare them for their roles.

3. **Find someone who** can tell you a story (or find an article online) about a "Trustee from Hell." What was the problem that trustee posed and how was it—or could it have been—resolved? No one intentionally accepts these demanding roles only to fail. We need trustees' help and they need ours. Again, jot some notes about how you can play a role in reducing these stumbling blocks.

4. **With trustees on** your side, you can do a lot more for your staff and your library than you can without them. List one initiative or activity that you can plan *right now* that will involve one or more members of your library's board. Build a bond and help each other succeed.

5. **Is there a** board in your community or in your library community that you might join? Look around for a good one (they all need supporters) and find out if and how you can get on it. Being a board member is one of the best ways you can come to understand other board members and how you can work better with them. What's your plan?

Success with Stakeholders

WEEK TWO | YOUR COMMUNITY

If you've never seen the old television shows *Green Acres* or *Petticoat Junction,* I would suggest you go watch a few DVDs of them, because I would argue that Sam Drucker's General Store was the first ever "Third Place." Now we talk about that like it's a big, complicated deal. Entire workshops are held on "How to Turn Your Library into a Third Place." For me and for Lisa Douglas (I'm telling you, get a DVD), you don't know what you're missing. It's simpler than all that.

It's all about community. Your library has to be the "general store" where everyone goes to do everything, to see everyone, to hear all, and perhaps most important, to leave their mark. If your customers are coming in just to pick out a book and leave, then, as the boss, you'd better get busy. You've got community-building to do. Here's how you can do it.

First of all, make sure your community knows you. Once a month, at the very least, you need to get out of your building and get involved in some local luncheon, service club meeting, presentation, or just a meeting to have a cup of coffee with someone. If you think your staff need you in the building more, you're only half right. Your staff do need you—but they need you *out* making friends and building relationships that will help support them in lean times and become the foundation of their large and efficient advocacy network.

But remember that there's a danger inherent in this "community-building" too. And that is, be careful you and your staff don't go too far . . . and enter into a dysfunctional, needy, or just plain unprofessional relationship with the townspeople that can end up bringing divisiveness and emotional distress down on you and your employees. Here's how that could end up happening.

There was once a manager who overdedicated herself to her involvement in the community. She belonged to just about every group that existed, she took leadership roles in each, requiring her (or, in reality, her staff) to do more "outside" work all the time, and she was forever at meetings or functions in support of these endeavors. In short, she was never there when you needed her. Or at least her attention was diverted away from her library more often than not. This didn't do anyone any good. Your first, foremost, and primary responsibility is to run a great library and to be a good boss. Look for opportunities, certainly, to promote and involve your library outside its walls, but always keep your heart with your staff and what they're doing.

There was another staff of a very small branch that, according to their manager, had practically adopted its customers. Their users were dedicated and extremely appreciative of the services offered in their "corner" of the world, and when substitutes from other buildings were sent there, they were treated as outsiders or worse. From a staffing and operational perspective, this was a nightmare. One woman customer went so far as to come in one day with cookies, hand them to the "new person," and admonish her to "not eat them but save them for 'her' librarians." Once, when a regular customer passed away, the entire staff sought permission to close the branch for the morning of the services, so they could all attend. When it was explained that this was impossible, a rift was caused that took months to heal.

So beware of the repercussions your community connections can inspire, but don't let that stop you from making them. As with everything about being a boss, this too calls for balance and professionalism. Combined with dedication to the success of the library, these components can help turn your library into a true "third place."

What's the secret to having the best of both worlds? Involve everyone! If you share the responsibility and rewards of local notoriety with your staff leaders, then everyone can win. Your staff can and should be known by a variety of community members, not just the ones who come to the Tuesday night programs. And by involving everyone, you then won't be pulled too far afield from your responsibilities, but will instead be developing your whole team as "movers and shakers" in their own right, as others get to know you all better.

By truly utilizing your "team," your community will get to know *all* of you better. You'll also be sharing and heralding the diverse, unique, individual gifts your staff members have to offer. What better way to grow connections? And finally, all of you will be effectively and professionally spreading the name and reputation of your library in a healthy and productive way, with enough time and energy left over to continue to move your library forward.

DON'T SEEK the LONE RANGER AWARD

Whether you're a brand-new boss or you've been around for a while and just haven't reached out into your community yet, you can't correct that on your own, nor should you. Remember, you've got a team . . . use them! Create strong ambassadors who understand how important they are to a strong library-community relationship. Use the "Four P's" model to get—and keep—them invested in this outreach.

Use the Four P's

- Explain the *purpose* of the library in the community
- Paint a *picture* of how the outcome of your success looks and feels
- Create a step-by-step *plan* to get there
- Give your staff a *part,* so they have a chance to contribute to the library's future[2]

WORKSHEET

1. **Identify the most** active groups or organizations in your community. Which ones really make a difference? Which are the ones featured in your local news most often? Those are the ones that have the real "movers and shakers" involved. List the groups, and then identify the top three.

2. **Now, looking at** those three, which ones involve interests about which you feel most strongly? To which would you have the most to contribute? The biggest mistake you can make is to become involved in the Historical Society if you don't enjoy working with older adults. Don't join the Chamber of Commerce if business issues bore you. If you love children and the schools, is the Board of Education on your list? Play to your strengths, so you can stay interested, as well as make a viable contribution to the group's efforts. Below, list your number one choice and everything you can find out about them. When do they meet? What do their minutes show you they've been focusing on? Who are the people involved? Take the time to actually write out how you will get involved.

3. **Now look at** the other two groups. What staff members might be good matches for them? Remember, these are "ambassadors" for the library you'll be sending out. Their enthusiasm and integrity are what matter here, not their titles. Write a couple of names down and then sketch out steps you'll take to get these people involved, on behalf of your library.

4. **Keep the rest** of your list handy. You don't have to start out at 100 percent, with every organization covered, but as you view and enjoy the success and rewards that the three of you will be accumulating, you're going to want to move more people into more places as time goes on. And don't be surprised when community leaders start calling *you,* as word of your library's commitment to the community starts to spread.

Success with Stakeholders

WEEK THREE | YOUR INDUSTRY PEERS

This book is the result of my friendship with a national library consultant and author whom I met when her husband sold my library our program registration software. Since then, she and I have stayed in touch and, most recently, co-presented at three national library conferences. At the most recent conference, I reconnected with another woman I admire who still works at my former library system. We ended up talking about similar interests, and next month she and I will copresent at another local library's staff day.

In short, my connections with my industry or library peers have shaped and continue to shape my career. It's been my library counterparts who have encouraged my development and, ultimately, helped my library to get the most out of me—and vice versa.

How about you? How involved are you in meeting others from neighboring libraries, or in meeting vendors or even students or teachers at your nearest library school? What are you giving back? Do you have a mentor from whom you learn or, better yet, are you mentoring someone else? You can't thrive if you live your professional life in a cocoon. You need to reach out to expand your abilities, to keep sharp for your own sake and for your customers, and continue to stretch beyond your limits.

So, how do you do that? Well, to start with, you can't overdo it. If you examine the alphabet soup of our library world, you'll see that we have local library networks, national networks, specialized groups within those networks, state organizations, and more. You are only one person and, don't forget, your staff need you too. Pick your interests. Or better yet, be open to them picking you, which is usually a reflection of your natural talents.

Another thing to remember (and it's okay if this is beginning to sound like a mantra): you can't do it alone!

Reflect for a minute on the richness of your library staff's skills and abilities. Think how energized people have been when they returned from an excellent meeting or workshop or conference. If you multiplied that energy times several people in your library, what might the cumulative result be? One guess—immeasurable.

Think of your industry as a resource for you and your team. Where else will you learn of the newest ideas, the brightest solutions, and the smartest practices to take back to help your staff? The more you can involve staff from your library outside of your four walls, the more you're going to know. Period. And then there's always the added possibility that once you're out there, you might make a contribution of your own as well.

What trends are right around your library's corner? How are libraries your size saving money—or finding money to help support them? Your circulation staff won't likely be the ones to get out there and find out. You're the boss. It's up to you to make sure that either you or other members of your team are well aware of what's around the next corner.

Our industry is only as strong as we make it, one by one. Look around at your local organizations. Every good idea is supported by some volunteer peer group, somewhere. Every new service is tested by an innovator. It's easy to tell everyone how busy you are and just stay "home." But, I challenge you, name three innovative, influential library leaders who did just that and still made a difference. Bet you can't. Now think of three local, state, or even national library leaders you do admire and whose accomplishments you'd like to emulate. It's time you and others within your library go find them. Get involved. Become part of what we can all do together.

AVOID the JOHN WAYNE SCHOOL of LEADERSHIP

What is effective leadership? Among the solutions . . . is shared leadership. This implies the concept that the management team takes on the responsibility for leadership . . . particularly when [they have] the expertise, experience or passion for a particular issue. The concept of shared leadership offers a way of increasing risk taking, innovation and commitment that can create an organization that is responsive, flexible and successful.[3]

WORKSHEET

1. **What networks or** groups or organizations exist that can help your library most directly? List them from local to national. Include pro and con notes for each. How could they make a difference for you? (Some of them can't.) Are they too expensive? Is too much travel involved? It's important to be realistic in your assessments. A promise to become involved in something you don't have the time or money for will just result in frustration on both your parts.

2. **Next, pick your** favorites. In which of those groups would you most like to become involved? Why? Which ones do you plan to avoid like the plague? Why? Pick two that would matter to your library and that would "work" within your operation.

3. **How can you** get started with your number one pick? Might you just join a committee, for starters? Chair a committee? Do they need professionals to teach a workshop for free or, at the very least, attend one? Find the name of a contact within your selection and call or e-mail them right now to get the ball rolling. Spend a minute writing out how you'll introduce yourself and what you have to offer.

4. **Now go back** to your original list. Remember, you're leading a team here. We already covered avoiding the "Lone Ranger" approach to success. Compare the list you created of intriguing networking organizations with your staff roster and match *them* up as well. Don't limit the value of networking professionally to just you—get as much of your staff out there as possible. That way, the impact you all return with will be greater and the library world—at least around your library—will know you and your staff have arrived! List some possible "leader-group" matches below. Then start talking to your team about the future.

Success with Stakeholders

WEEK FOUR | YOUR STAFF LEADERS

It's true. It's lonely at the top. You're going to be making a lot of unpopular decisions. You're going to be introducing "new" services that many staff members won't like. You're going to have to champion change in a culture that often prefers the status quo (because they know how to succeed in it). And you're going to have to discipline everyone's favorite employee, at least once. You're going to need some friends and some support. You're going to need your team. You've already worked through several examples demonstrating the need to utilize the strengths of others on your staff in the library, in the community, and in the industry. You may already have a strong team with which to begin working, or you may have stepped into a quagmire. Either way, you and your library can still be successful.

Whether you're a brand-new boss or one who has been around for a while, there's no time like the present to start building those talented people around you into the strength of your organization. To build your team, you need to do several things. You begin by getting to know them and them you. Then you work on identifying your library's real leaders and developing relationships with them that make a difference. Don't *ever* think it's too late. Today is a new day.

Did you notice the above emphasis on the word *real*? That's because you can't always tell the leaders by their titles. Normally, you'll have some level of support staff around you. You'll need to develop a mutually respectful, professional relationship with them in order to move forward effectively. You'll notice again that I didn't say *friendship,* I said *professional relationship.* There's a difference. Here's an explanatory analogy in terms of lunch. In a "friendship," you can go out to lunch every week with only the person you like the most . . . your friend from years back. In a "professional relationship," you can go out with her only in a group and not every day . . . you have to leave everyone some time to vent about *you*!

Sometimes you and the members of your leadership team may not even like one another. Liking each other is a bonus, but it's not necessarily a requirement. So for now and for the sake of your library, you all need to work together to get the job done. So how do you do that? Think contact, communication, and cooperation. You have to accept that you're facing the same challenges and want the same outcomes. Then you need a consensus of support to try out your solutions.

Structure can be your friend in this process. First, establish a monthly meeting schedule and try to stick to it. These should be individual, one-on-one meetings that you regularly have with each person on your team. Keep a binder for each person as well, and as questions or issues arise in between your meetings, stick them in the binder so they don't fall through the cracks.

Use your meetings to ask what's going well, what's not, and (most important) how you can help each other. This forthright communication and sharing of concerns will help for a strong bond that will serve you both well. Talk, talk, talk, and then talk some more.

Remember too that if you expect support from your staff leaders, they need to know what you're doing and what you're thinking as well. Tell them your reasons for everything. Share your philosophy. A good rule of thumb is that staff, while on a one-floor elevator ride, should be able to succinctly answer the question "What's your boss all about, anyway?"

So how do you get to know your leaders and vice versa? Just as you're making your opinions and intent clear, you need to take the time to get to know them and their vision as well. People respond to honest caring. There's no secret formula. There's no big mystery. So to be a *really* good boss, you need to make connections and keep them sharp.

But I'm sure some of you are thinking, wait a minute, what about at my library? We're unionized!

It doesn't matter.

Whether your staff are organized formally or informally, there will still be leaders and followers and you'll still need to share as much with all of them as you can. The definition, I've been told, of a good boss is someone who gets work out of other people. That applies to you and it also applies to all the supervisors on your team.

Develop them. Work well with them. Respect them.

You'll notice that this section is entitled "Staff Leaders." In large part, the people on whom bosses come to depend are in leadership positions—but not always. As much as is possible within your organization, include members of your front line in your "leadership team." They will bring to your group's table a unique and unfiltered impression of the ideas you're considering and they'll keep you honest at the same time.

A word of warning, though: be careful about inappropriate relationships with staff that might be misconstrued as favoritism or—worse yet—cliques. Can you still go out to lunch with the people you've worked closely alongside all these years? Sure! As long as you're in a group. Or if you feel the need for one-on-one sessions, be sure you do that with everyone, not just a chosen few.

It doesn't have to be lonely at the top all the time. Some final decisions will be yours alone, but along the way you'll need a team around you on whom you can depend and trust. You'll all go further together than you would alone.

"Average managers play checkers, while great managers play chess."

A great manager figures out who's the knight, the queen, the pawn. She takes those very different abilities and contributions into the service of the overall plan. She then builds a *team* out of individuals.

To do this, we must learn as much about the individuals we manage as possible. We need to know about their

- Strengths and weaknesses
- Skills
- Temperament
- Areas of interest
- Motivators
- Personal goals
- Ideas of fun and what they find boring
- Life stressors
- Family
- Time management style
- Organizational abilities
- Learning style[4]

WORKSHEET

1. **You're going to** need to remove roadblocks, to appreciatively praise, and to intuitively grow your leadership staff at all times. In order to do all that, you'll have to also keep in touch with what's going on in their world. What's keeping them up at night? Set up a monthly meeting schedule right now with each and every employee who reports to you. See Bill on the first Tuesday of each month at 2:00 p.m. See Julie on the third Monday at noon. Keep going. Do it now. You can change these dates and times, certainly, as can they, but by putting them down on paper (or in something like Outlook's Calendar) you are legitimizing your intent and each person's value to you.

2. **If you don't** have them already, start a three-ring binder for each person you supervise. You can keep a pocket folder for "save" items—things you'll want to see again come evaluation time. And you can keep a log of what you discuss at your monthly meetings (and check off the "to-dos" when they're done). Also, as things come up during each month that can wait but must be addressed, this binder will be the perfect place to store them. What does all this accomplish, other than satisfying the office supplies lover in us all? Again, on the appearances side, it legitimizes your intent to work professionally and strategically with each leader while, on the practical side, it helps you do just that. It's a win-win situation.

3. **Form a "library** leadership team." If you don't already have a "managers' group," or even if you do but you want to make it more effective, form a library leadership team that will meet monthly with you and be a support system. A word of advice: shake things up a bit. Don't just put people whose titles or pay grades separate them from the rest of the staff on board, but let them help you identify other "leaders" whom you can bring in. Be creative. Set lofty goals. And most of all, establish a clear charge and format for this group. State in writing what its members will do, how long members should serve, and how they are replaced. Then get this energized group together and get out of their way!

4. **Create your library** leadership team's first meeting date, agenda, and invitation and attach them to this exercise. Good luck, and enjoy the new strength, energy, and promise this team will bring to your library!

Staffing

WEEK ONE | HIRING AND FIRING

Entire libraries could be filled with all the books written on the topics of hiring and firing. Still, the single most inspirational hiring concept that I've heard in twenty-five years doesn't involve what you might expect to find in those books. It's not about how to do behavioral interviewing (although that is critical). It's not about performing drug and background checks (but don't skip those). It *is* about finding and keeping only the best.

It tells us we should accept *only* greatness. It's about great staffing at *all* levels. Just as collection development isn't just about buying books, but is also about weeding them, this idea does not just cover only hiring staff, but also helping the wrong people move on and developing the ones you keep. It's about who you hire, who you keep, and who you let go. Or, in the words of Jim Collins in *Good to Great and the Social Sectors,* it's about doing "whatever you can to get the right people on the bus, the wrong people off the bus and the right people into the right seats."[1]

The best part is that any boss can do this. Jim Collins explained that Colorado high school teacher Roger Briggs applied this principle when he decided he *could* change the culture of the department he ran. How did he do it? He demanded greatness and he accepted nothing less. Collins explains that Briggs "began to view the first three years of a teacher's career as an extended interview."[2] He also completely changed the standard, all but expected three-year tenure track from "'Yes, you'll likely get tenure, unless you've done something egregious' to a default of 'No, you will most likely *not* get tenure, unless you have proven yourself to be an exceptional teacher.'"[3]

A critical part of his process was an honest, ongoing evaluation of each employee for their first few months and the honest understanding that if they did not prove themselves to be exceptional, they wouldn't be staying. Collins explains further that "early assessment mechanisms turn out to be more important than hiring mechanisms. There is no perfect interviewing technique, no ideal hiring method; even the best executives make hiring mistakes. You can only know for certain about a person by working with that person."[4]

So picture yourself at the decision-making point of your hiring process. If you have two *good* candidates from whom to choose, whether they be internal or external, my (and Collins's) advice to you would be . . . repost! Don't hire, don't retain, and don't settle for *good*. Insist on *great*. Teach yourself and your other hiring supervisors not to tolerate anything less in your staff than greatness and, seat by seat, you'll turn your bus around too!

Here's one way to apply *great* guidelines when making hires. At my library, we truly believe the *attitude* of our staff is more important than their skills. Not that skill doesn't matter, because it does. But in our particular search for greatness, we feel attitude matters more. So we "scan" for that. We have no reference desks at my library and no circulation desk. We support our customers' success in using their library by having staff all around, out on the floor, to help whenever and wherever needed.

We understand that it takes a special staff member to make this approach work, so more than once we've "prescreened" applicants *just* to check their attitude, their approach to working with others, and their communication skills. How? In groups, we've asked them to work together doing everything from building a bridge out of rolled-up newspapers to writing a rhyming answering machine message to explain the library's closing on Groundhog Day.

Try whatever works for you. If your staff like to have fun (and they should, because, if not, why is everyone getting up in the morning?), then have fun with the activities. Let your applicant see the type of library you really are—and find out who they really are—behind their resume—as well.

As one expert explained, "It's about learning to recognize and identify those qualities that drive individuals to succeed . . . optimism, empathy, persuasiveness. Forget about hiring for experience and hire based on that optimism, persistence and resilience that come through in a positive way."[5]

Remember, your goal is to make sure that, in the end, the person you are bringing on board is the right person for your culture, the best person for the job, and the greatest person for your library.

No discussion about hiring would be complete without a note on hiring for diversity. If you don't know that this means more than how many colors of the rainbow are represented on your staff, then admit you are ready to learn more about this important facet of organizational success. Do you have a policy for ensuring that you have all kinds of people contributing to your success, and then make sure everyone follows that policy? If you don't, then start working on your director or your board and get one written. You don't need to read a list of the values that staff of many different ages, backgrounds, cultures, races, orienta-

---

Richard Rubin, dean of Kent State University's School of Library and Information Science and a renowned expert on HR issues, outlined seven key principles for successful staff management:

1. *Principle of organizational survival*—Help accomplish organizational goals by managing people properly. Unfortunately, views people as means to an end. Mitigated by next principle.
2. *Principle of individuality*—People are important as individuals and must be afforded attention and respect even when organizational ends may be affected. Manifest in benefit programs, privacy, no mandating [that] all think the same.
3. *Principle of consistency*—You can't apply rules in an arbitrary fashion. You will lose the confidence and respect of your employees. Being consistent often interferes with being fair.
4. *Principle of fairness*—Where consistency demands uniform application of rules and regulations, fairness demands that the rules themselves be just and justly applied.
5. *Principle of legal responsibility*—Personnel policies and practices must remain firmly within the bounds of the law, and no individual in authority should be permitted to order or encourage an employee to commit an unlawful act.
6. *Principle of happiness*—A personnel system should promote the greatest happiness for the greatest number. So policies [are] designed to maximize job satisfaction within a context that allows the organization to accomplish its goals.
7. *Principle of ethical action*— Examples of ethical breaches: privacy, misuse of authority, organizational inadequacies.[6]

---

tions, and lifestyles can add to your library. Everyone knows that. What most people don't know is how to find that mix.

Here's one simple and foolproof idea to follow. Stop and look over every interview pool before the first appointments are set. Is diversity reflected in the pool? If not, then what does that tell you about the odds of adding diversity to your staff? Make sure that every opportunity to add a new employee also offers an opportunity to diversify. Maybe that means finding a name in your "B" pile and moving it over to "A." Try it. You'll be surprised what you might have missed.

After the new person comes on board, your job is far from finished. Not all hires turn out well, to no one's particular credit or blame. If yours isn't going so well, you should know that your leadership is needed at this point more than ever. You have to fix it. Firing is to hiring as weeding is to collection development. One is really just as important as the other. Even though you may not want to, sometimes you just have to do it. You can be left with no other choice. Just be certain that you've tried the other choices earlier, and they didn't work. But it's never easy when you are negatively affecting the life of another human being. There are ways to ensure that your firings, which you will have, are the best they can be.

First, don't let it get personal. Although you must always maintain your own and your employee's dignity, you, as the boss, must also keep a professional distance and viewpoint. Don't use conversation that makes it about the person. For example, instead of "You haven't been doing your job well," perhaps "The library needs a different kind of performance from the person in your position." It's not about you versus them. It's about what's best for your library. Always, always leave the person with his dignity intact.

Second, be able to honestly say, "I did absolutely everything humanly possible to help this person turn himself around and succeed." Then make sure that's true. Use frequent meetings, clear goal setting, fair and enforced improvement deadlines, applicable training opportunities, and perhaps even counseling to improve the situation. Do everything you can. In the end, the best you can do is to say "we tried to avoid separation" and mean it.

Popeye was right: "I y'am what I y'am." The most common—and fatal—hiring mistake is to find someone with the right skills but the wrong mind-set and hire them on the theory, "We can change 'em."[7]

Firing is one of the most difficult things a boss can do. But don't avoid it. You can cause immeasurable, irreparable damage to your staff by dodging making that tough decision and leaving the wrong person in the wrong place. Everyone else depends on your decision-making in these situations.

So try to resolve the issues, try to improve the performance, and if that doesn't work, be the boss and make the tough call.

Then, with the position open, review everything you can find on hiring the *right* person and try again!

Suggested Reading

Collins, Jim. *Good to Great and the Social Sectors: Why Business Thinking Is Not the Answer.* Boulder, CO: HarperCollins, 2005.

WORKSHEET

1. **Most frequently, bosses** don't review their interview questions until the applicant is almost at the doorstep. That's too late to realize how old and "dated" they seem or that they're not going to tell you what you need to know. Find the most recent interview questions in your files and review them, *but first,* list here the qualities you hope to identify when interviewing. Then, toss the questions that don't apply.

2. **Think of at** least three other ways, besides using a traditional interview, that you can gain valuable insight about potential employees. It's okay to get help with this one. Remember what you learned in your first library class . . . the reference librarian's best resource is the telephone. Call a couple of experienced bosses and ask for advice.

3. **All of the** above work applies to new staff you'll be adding. Now take a look at your existing staff and, first, list the ones with the best attitude below. Then list those who could use some coaching. Do you see the obvious? Outline a staff-mentoring program that will bring them together. (Remember to articulate your goal for this program clearly, so everyone involved takes it as seriously as they need to.)

Staffing

WEEK TWO | EVALUATING AND DEVELOPING

No matter how hard you look, you'll never find anyone who really, really likes their evaluation tool. Some parse the job description, some give letter grades, some give numbers, and others go all the way back to kindergarten-style "acceptable or unacceptable" ratings.

None of these methods gives your employees a really clear, objective measurement of how they're doing. They can't. They're subjective forms being filled out with subjective opinions often months after the performance took place. Libraries using a 1–5 scale, for example, have a hard time explaining clearly why, when people think they're doing everything that's asked of them, they get a "3." They think they deserve better than a "C" or an average grade. But when you think about it, achieving all that's asked of you, nothing more or less, would be just "acceptable." But who wants to be called that?

Worse yet, if your evaluation system is connected to pay raises in a merit design, you'll find even more resistance to your own or your supervisors' personal interpretations of staff members' performance.

None of the designs or measurements or checkmarks or red star systems really matters when you consider the purpose of evaluations. They exist to improve performance and to allow for rational, documented separation, if necessary. So, then, what *does* matter when bosses evaluate staff?

Honesty. Whatever period of time is being evaluated, *everything* that has happened during that time needs to be included. If a staff member was coached about customer service complaints early in the year, and then didn't have any more complaints for many months, that doesn't mean you leave the incident out. Rather, you have to find a way to positively comment on the improvement demonstrated, while still documenting the original problem. Why? Because the problem might return and you might not still be there when it does. How can a new boss deal with a recurring issue when it was never documented in the first place? Or, if you are there, even you would be hard-pressed to make a case for discipline if it looks like a single event.

Thoroughness. As was suggested earlier, keep a folder for each and every person you supervise so that, when the time comes to write an evaluation, it really just writes itself as you compile comments about your collection of materials. We've all suffered through evaluations that were written within the hour before the meeting. It's no secret what that feels like. Don't do it. You pay your staff members a salary, but that's not where their compensation stops. Every person deserves a special time set aside once a year to sit down and listen to her boss's recognition of her achievements. Her boss's *thorough* recognition is what makes it real. So by using your file, you won't have to say "Debbie shows great customer service." Instead, dig into your paperwork and find something you can use for substantiation. If you have copies of notes you've received about the employee, use them. Say, "Three customers wrote letters during this past year, complimenting Debbie on outstanding customer service behaviors she showed, such as great communication skills, problem solving, and a positive attitude." Now that's a real evaluation!

Fairness. I'm always a little nervous before my evaluation, which is really kind of silly, since I should know and expect every single thing that will be in it. Evaluations should *never* include surprises, nor any comment or criticism that has not been discussed before. Even in a world where nobody promised us fairness, that's just not fair. If there are existing performance issues, make sure you deal with them on the spot, as they arise, complete with clear expectations for improvement, so that the evaluation period remains a "review," as it is supposed to be. Document those instances and use them to clearly make your case in the evaluation.

Face-to-face. Finally, the conversation surrounding an evaluation inarguably matters the most. This is when you can be frank, and perhaps even a bit more detailed than you want to be in writing, given the permanence of the document. This is where you can set goals (which will later be written down), and this is where you can ask for feedback on *your* performance as a boss so the end result of this exercise is that both you and your employee grow and improve. Talk to your employee. And listen. This is a development experience for both of you.

The performance evaluation is a development tool. Make sure you never use it for any other reason. It's not a disciplinary exercise, nor an empty, glad-handing pat on the back.

EVERY GREAT BOSS'S TOP TEN TIPS for EXCELLENT PERFORMANCE EVALUATIONS

1. Be honest
2. Be consistent
3. Have a sound foundation
4. Be encouraging
5. Support it
6. Get it (pre-)reviewed for clarity
7. Be hopeful, with reason
8. Present it well
9. Allow for (real) feedback
10. Revisit it[8]

Staff members want and expect and need regular honest, open discussions about what's expected of them, how they're doing, and how they can improve. Don't skip your opportunity to give them that. You'll be busy. Deadlines for evaluations will come and go. Pretty soon you'll be reading an exit interview and, to the question "Were you fairly evaluated?" the answer will be "I haven't had an evaluation in three years!"

It's up to you. Whether you are a new boss or an experienced one, if you haven't done so already, set up a calendar, establish deadlines and expectations for your other supervisors to do the same, optimize your forms and systems, and ensure that these valuable development tools are part of your library's life. What's the payoff? Your staff will improve, and feel truly appreciated, and you will be a better boss.

Another critical development tool that you cannot overlook is development from day one. If you don't already have an effective and compelling orientation system in place, you better get one started. The best plans include worksheets that will help you introduce your new staff to the organization, as well as help ensure that supervisors under you are doing the same for theirs.

Chart the orientation through dates, for example, "by the end of the first week" or "by the end of the first month." This also helps ensure you're not overloading your new person, but introducing policies, practices, and operational instructions in a time-released way, only when they really need them. Make sure you all follow the checklist, perhaps even requiring that, once complete, it be signed off and kept in everyone's personnel folder.

WORKSHEET

1. **How long has** it been since you've had an evaluation? No matter, think back to the last one and list below the best (left) and worst (right) features it contained. Remember, you can learn as much from bad examples as from good ones.

2. **Many bosses will** send out questions for an employee to answer about herself before writing that person's evaluation. These can be very helpful in clarifying your understanding of the employee's challenges and goals. Questions might include, for example, "What was the high point of your last year?" or "What training do you most wish you could have soon? Why?" Below, write at least five other probing things you might ask and then, when you do your next few evaluations, try sending the questions out first.

3. **Look over the** evaluation tool your library is currently using. Do some research. There are articles and books on outstanding techniques and designs you could try. Draw up just a simple draft of how your library's evaluation tool might be improved and begin circulating it among your staff to get some feedback. Remember, if you have access to other bosses around you, ask for their insights as well.

Staffing

WEEK THREE | SCHEDULING

Here's the most important thing to remember about your schedule. You're bigger than it is. Putting people's names down on a piece of paper is not just about arranging work. It's about arranging life. You are in control, and with the right priorities and practices in place, scheduling can be fun!

I'm not crazy. I really mean this. Scheduling should be fun, flexible, fair, mechanical, and fast. Remember this: there's the schedule (at some point, at least, just a piece of paper) and then there's you. You're bigger. If you are spending more than thirty minutes a week getting a new week's schedule ready, then you're doing it wrong. Or, worse yet, if you are one of those bosses who freaks out when someone comes to you with a request for a change because "I just finished that schedule! What do you want me to do, make it up all over again?" then you're wrong again.

You remember the story from earlier in this workbook about the boss who wouldn't change the schedule so her staff member could spend time with her son before he left for two years in the service?! That's a true story, and I'm sure you've been part of or heard of many others just like it.

Now, don't get me wrong. I'm not suggesting that you strive to give everyone what they want so you can be their best friend. There's a difference here. I'm suggesting that while you "own" a certain number of hours of everyone's life each week, you can and should treat that time like the valuable commodity that it is.

So how do you do that and still keep the needs of the library (always paramount) first? Simple. You use structure and planning. You invest initial time to create a system that works and then, in response to the lives that your staff members lead, you can make simple, fair, and fast changes that work.

Spend your time up-front to create an effective framework for a reasonable rotation of shifts. If your staff members are expected to work every other weekend, then you'll need two schedules' skeletons to accommodate that, one for week "A" and one for week "B." Or, if your staff is so large that everyone only works one

SCHEDULES PLAN LIVES, NOT JUST WORK

You and your staff *both* need to keep a balance between work obligations and non-work life opportunities. Happy and productive professionals are careful to organize their work so that "their successful careers are matched only by their satisfying personal lives."[9]

Consider . . .

- Disney CEO Michael Eisner, who refused to work late if he'd made a commitment to his children
- Columbia TriStar Motion Pictures vice chairman Lucy Fisher, whose four-day schedule lets her dedicate Fridays to her family
- Telecommunications mogul John Malone, who works just five hours a day but who usually drives home for lunch
- Even Jill Barad, Mattel's hard-driving CEO and president, who ritualistically watches *ER* and *The X-Files* with her husband and sons[10]

weekend a month, you'll create "A," "B," "C," and "D" schedules. These are going to take some time. There's no shortcut here. For each week, you have to insert your full-timers, then your part-timers, then note meetings, holidays, and so on. But every minute you spend in creation (and in updating, which you'll probably do at least twice a year) will be worth the week-after-week benefit of a fifteen-minute schedule prep.

People will leave and new staff will arrive. Class schedules for your student staff members will shift with semesters or, worse, you will lose staff due to other, more permanent issues. For a good boss, these fluctuations will be met with no more angst than a misrouted phone call. For others, though, staff will tread lightly to their door to announce a babysitter or class change, fearing the wrath and reaction they'll likely receive. Which boss do you want to be?

Remember, the schedule is just a piece of paper. The staff, well, those are real people.

A few words of schedule warning, though, for those new to influencing the lives and challenges others face. First, don't park people somewhere and leave them there for too long. As much as is possible, move your staff around so that you can help keep their perspective open and their sense of teamwork broad. Too much time spent in one location, department, or branch can lead to a dysfunction that undermines library service at best and fosters an unhealthy and unprofessional, misguided loyalty at worst. If everyone works for your library system, then they should be scheduled, from time to time, all around it. You can build a strong and valuable sense of camaraderie with this approach, or develop a fearful and suspicious attitude towards "outsiders" without it. And you might just end up being one of those outsiders.

Finally, if you expect your staff to have flexible schedules, so that they're ready to help the library when and where they're needed, then build flexibility into their schedule on a consistent basis. Don't schedule someone for Tuesday nights for fifteen years, and then be surprised when, after being switched to Wednesday nights, they balk.

Family, educational commitment, and other life demands are critical to consider when scheduling. Make sure you have mastered the mechanics of creating schedules, so these more important issues can be addressed. But always, always keep the needs of the library first, and make sure your staff know and experience that reality all the time.

"Sorry to hear you're not feeling well today. Don't worry about coverage; I'll take care of it. See you tomorrow." The master of the schedule speaks!

WORKSHEET

1. **How much time** do you spend creating your schedule? Or how much time do the people you supervise spend? If it's less than one hour per week, then you can skip this question and go on to the next. If it's more, then take out a sheet of paper now and start creating drafts. There are plenty of books and tools out there to use. Create rotations. Pretend no one is on vacation or at a meeting or sick. Once you've gotten everyone penciled in for their hours, duplicate the pages and work from them. One week at a time, just input the "events" that need to take place and make adjustments. Be fair and be consistent. (Attach your worksheets to this page, so you can revisit what you did the next time you update your drafts.) Then plan a special "Scheduling" workshop for your other supervisors and teach them to do the same. In the space below, sketch out your agenda or "plan of attack" for that meeting.

2. **How comfortable are** your staff members in asking for schedule changes? Do you have fair rules in place, including procedures and forms for requests off? The easier you make it to adjust a schedule, the more likely your staff will begin to balance their home and work life, which will ultimately benefit your library. If you don't have written guidelines for this yet, draft some out now and then work with your boss or your supervisors and devise a plan.

3. **Think back and** write down below the time you've taken off during the past twelve months. Have you enjoyed life? Have you missed important family events? How much time do you have on the books right now? Take the time to actually write down when you'll take time during the next six months or so and get it scheduled. Work to live, don't live to work.

4. **Finally, send out** an e-mail to your staff asking this one simple question: "If you could change one thing about our scheduling procedures, what would it be?" As the answers come back in, note the main points from their comments below, and then make sure you take their answers to heart and establish the fairest and most "family-friendly" schedule process you can—for the benefit of all.

Staffing

WEEK FOUR | MENTORING AND MOTIVATING

How high do you hold the bar for your staff, motivation-wise? Motivation, it can be argued, is a self-fulfilling prophecy, so take a look around and see exactly what level of expectation you've set for everyone. Is it high enough? Are they being challenged? Do you always expect more, expect the best, and expect to be surprised? If not, you're missing an opportunity and you're wasting time and talent. So why not raise it up a notch?

Consider this, then. In Europe, soccer fans are expected to be rowdy and even violent at the really big matches. And they often live up to those expectations. Bleachers are crushed in the frenzy of the sport, and sometimes fans even die. The behavior is just what is expected, so no one is surprised.

But what about in golf? Consider fans at the Masters, one of golf's most prestigious and exciting tournaments. Based on the public's expectations for golfing fans, we have a very different idea about how the 25,000 people in attendance at the Sunday final round will behave. Not only will the masses be held in place by a single, lightweight cloth rope stretched behind the green, but at the same time, they will stand absolutely still and quiet. That's what the world "expects" from golf fans.

So how about at your library or in your department? What's the expectation? How high do you set the bar? Do you tolerate backbiting, gossip, and whining? Is hand-wringing and casting blame okay, or do you prefer problem solving, positivity, and professionalism? If it's the former, then you need to be aware of the negative motivational effects those activities will have on even your most upbeat employees. Or do you model a positive, caring, and professional approach to all interactions, both those between staff and customers and between coworkers as well? Mentoring can be as direct as a conversation across a table or as indirect as how staff *see* you behave toward their coworkers and supervisors. But how else can you mentor and motivate your staff toward higher standards? Here are a few tips that might make a difference.

FAIL FAST

An hour of experimenting and action learning is worth more than a hundred hours of polarizing speculation and debate.

If we have no choice about whether we'll encounter failure, we have two options: fail slow or fail fast.

Innovation leaders choose the latter.

This translates into experimenting with ideas more often. Instead of talking or thinking or planning them on paper, take your ideas before they're fully formed and *try them out* in the field. The lessons you'll learn will give you not only quicker results, but *better* results.[11]

Dream big.

Most of us have heard of BHAGs (big, hairy, audacious goals) and how motivating they can be. They're out there, they're almost unattainable, and they're sometimes silly they are so immense. But they work. I do a lot of public speaking and workshops now, but back in 1987 I had a manager who suggested that I take over as co-leader of a five-week library literacy class. "Me?" I asked her. "You've got to be kidding! I could *never* speak in front of people! You'd better get someone else to do it." But maybe because she saw something in me and maybe because she didn't have anyone else available, she stood firm. She told me I had the right attitude for the job and I just needed a little experience. Then she paired me up with an extremely polished facilitator and she sent me to several training opportunities to study how adults learn, how to create presentations, and how to be an effective speaker. Her dreams for her staff were big, but she knew it would take more than dreams to succeed, so she supported all of our growing with real-life learning. This year, I gave a presentation to over 500 people. Audacious! I couldn't have done it without her.

Be trusting.

Once you've found the targets for which your staff members will reach and you've gotten them as much help and support as possible, trust that they'll make it the rest of the way themselves. Good bosses actually count on initial mistakes and use them to keep staff moving forward. Whatever you do, don't let a small failure end someone's progress. Rather than leaving us feeling foolish or worse, incompetent, failure should embolden us and convince us that we've figured out one more piece of the puzzle and we're almost there . . . success-wise. As I've already mentioned, "No mistake is final!"

Sing praises.

Don't be phony when you praise or reward your staff for their achievements. There is nothing *less* motivating than false praise. But neither should you hold back on letting them or the entire staff hear and know about all their small achievements along the way to developing their careers. We thrive on the success of those we admire as much as we do on our own. Be sure everyone knows all of each other's "growth" stories. Not only will each person appreciate the encouragement that will result, but overall the brand of your staff will be growth, resilience, and development. Success is contagious.

Be the proof.

While allowing kids to sleep, unbelted, in the backseat during the 1950s and '60s, most parents would drive cross-country while smoking with the windows rolled up. Then they'd tell us to be careful and take care of ourselves. What is one of the most frequently heard explanations for these contradictions? "Do what I say, not what I do." Well, that never really worked at home and it's sure not going to work for your staff.

Without sounding too philosophical, it was Gandhi who said, "Be the change you want to see in the world." Now, that *will* work with your staff. Like it or not, you're the boss and they look up to you. Have you worked for someone who screamed about attendance, but was always late to work and meetings? How about someone who preached good customer service and communication skills, but then flew off the handle and screamed at staff in front of customers, whenever she felt things weren't going her way? The message here? How about something a little less politically careful: "The fish stinks from the head down."

You, as the boss, will set the tone for your library, whether you want to or not and whether you like it or not. So motivate your staff the way you would want to be motivated (or, if you're lucky, like you were motivated). Encourage them, and their work will encourage you. Support them, and their success will support you. This particular week's topic is ripe with clichés. But here's perhaps the simplest yet truest direction for mentoring and motivation: do unto others.

Be clear. I met a manager from a western state whose library was on a downhill slide. There had been several changes in bosses recently and, as a result, all of the keys to success mentioned earlier—dreaming, trusting, praising—had fallen by the wayside. In their

Appreciative leadership expert Jack Ricchiuto says we need to debunk the "common mythology" that is based on negativity and replace it with really believing in our staff.

"Don't spend time in your organization talking about

> . . . What we don't have, don't want, don't like, can't do, what's wrong, what's not working, our weakness, gaps, and our inconsistencies and failures.

Rather, success comes from knowing

> . . . Our strengths, learning from our successes, and engaging what we *have* in the creation of what attracts us . . . what we dream.

The role of the appreciative leader is to

> . . . Inspire passion, discover opportunities and engage strengths."[12]

place, everyone was doing everyone else's job. Supervisors didn't know to whom to turn, since more than one administrator was asking them questions. Input, often conflicting, was coming from all directions and, worse, no one was devoting their full attention productively to their own assignments.

Establish responsibilities within your department or branch or system, and then motivate your staff by trusting them to do their job. Sure, accountability, communication, teamwork, and all the rest will play a part in your library's success but, above all, give your staff a chance to make the system work. Dream big and be surprised at what you can all accomplish.

Suggested Reading

Ricchiuto, Jack. *Collaborative Creativity: Unleashing the Power of Shared Thinking.* Winchester, VA: Oak Hill, 1996.

WORKSHEET

1. **List below the** names of each person you directly supervise. Next to each name, write one BHAG (big, hairy, audacious goal) that you feel both matches their passion and would greatly benefit your library. In your next meeting, talk to them about giving it a try (and how you would help). Most important, make sure they really know you believe they can do it!

2. **List the past** ten mistakes you've made most recently. Next to each, write what you think you learned from each. This is another good tool to keep in your "Next Meeting" folder. (You should have one of those for all staff who report to you.) The lesson will be that it's okay to make mistakes, as long as you keep learning from them. Many people are actually motivated by just having the chance to fix errors.

3. **Finally, what was** the one risk you wanted to take recently, but didn't? What potential success did you miss out on? Why did you hesitate? How can you try it now? Make sure you never stop motivating yourself.

MONTH 4

Communication

WEEK ONE | ANY WAY YOU CAN

Say something. Write something. Talk with your actions. Given a position where the decisions you make can and do affect the lives of others around you, your communication skills can be your crowning achievement or your tragic downfall. It's true that if no one was in the woods, there would be no sound when the tree fell. You're the boss. Do something. Then make sure everyone knows what you're doing. That's rule number one.

Your staff members have a right to hear from you. That's one reason you have to communicate well. It's part (a big part) of your job. That's reason number two. The list could go on and on. But, put simply, you want to be successful, your staff members want to be successful, and *all* of that hinges on great communication. So what are your options?

You can communicate your interest with just your presence. This is often called MBWA, or "Management by Walking Around." Believe it or not, there are libraries where front-line staff don't even *see* the boss for months at a time. Sometimes, when there's a back staff entrance near the parking lot that connects directly to the offices, most have to trust that their phantom leader really does arrive and leave every day, but in a court of law, they couldn't swear to it. Then there are the bosses who fly through the library on their way to someplace obviously more important, taking enough time to stop and complain about something but not to say hello to anyone.

"The idea is in order to stay in touch with the people who report directly to you simply walk around, talk to them, share with them, observe them, and don't be critical. If you do this with all your employees on a regular basis, you will quickly identify where they are succeeding, where they are struggling, and where they need help."[1]

Great bosses can and should be seen anywhere and everywhere. Remember when Barack Obama first moved into the White House? After just a few short weeks, he went down to the basement pressroom, surprising the press corps, just to see what it was like down there. When were you last seen somewhere other than your office? *What you do* communicates a lot!

If you don't think that *what you say,* whether in written or spoken form, matters just as much as what you do, I have two words for you—Sarah Palin. This is not a political comment. It's a fact. I don't think anybody, searching in the years to come for the best example of the value of speaking clearly, will look any further than *Saturday Night Live*'s ability to build a popular comedy skit *using Palin's own verbatim comments.* We don't roll out of the crib knowing how to communicate clearly. But you're the boss now, so you're out of excuses to not learn.

Whether you're speaking to a department meeting involving five longtime friends or to a city gathering of a hundred strangers, you *are* the library. How you look, what you say, how you say it, and ultimately, what you mean will affect your library and everyone who works for you. There are a lot of simple tips you'll pick up as you develop this skill, such as *don't ever wear anything that is more interesting than what you have to say,* or *don't ad-lib; it rarely works.* But there's a lot more serious and professional advice out there, in the form of books, training seminars, and seasoned experts, that you had better find.

How you develop your communication skills is up to you. Maybe you already have them and that's how you got to be the boss. What *is* irrefutable is that you better make sure to sharpen them and, most important, to *use* them. People both inside and outside your library need to hear your vision and understand it in order to follow you. You, as the boss, must communicate the success you want to see for your library.

I look back fondly on a comment one of the branch managers I supervise made after reading of a particularly challenging incident that took place within the library and how it was handled. She said as soon as she read the incident report that she knew exactly what I would say about it. To be able to predict my reaction so well, I think, is good. That means they hear me and they know my message.

So once you communicate—verbally or textually—what will your staff hear? If you consider (and you should) personality indicators such as Myers-Briggs or the Enneagram, you'll learn an important lesson. Your message will come through differently for different people with different styles of learning and various personality traits, and therefore they'll *hear* different things. You can use that to your advantage. Study how your staff differ. Learn the various ways to reach each of them and put all the skills you master to use. The biggest single communication mistake is to say nothing. The second biggest is to say something only one way, and expect everyone to hear and understand it the same way.

Cesar Millan is called "the Dog Whisperer" and he claims to be able to tell a lot about communication because of his special connection to these wonderful animals.

- *Trust your instincts.* Animals don't care about words. They recognize that what's really going on in any interaction is beneath the surface. Many of us have lost touch with this all-important, instinctual part of our nature. By paying attention to nonverbal cues, such as body language and energy, we can learn more about our friends, our loved ones, and ourselves.

and . . .

- *Be direct and consistent in your communication.* Many of my clients only intermittently enforce rules, leaving their pets confused about what is and isn't acceptable behavior. Great relationships, no matter the species, begin with clear and consistent communication.[2]

WORKSHEET

1. **Of all the** different types of communication, from walking around to listening to speaking and writing, list the three you would most like to improve. Now sketch out a plan to begin those improvements. Yes, today. Be realistic. Attending a master's program in London probably won't work. Under each entry, list at least three things you can *really* do to start being a better communicator.

2. **Communication starts at** the top, no doubt, but it doesn't stop there. In order to have a really healthy system, *all* of your supervisors need to have good communication skills. Below, list each person who reports to you and, next to their name, at least one thing you can help them do to improve their communication skills as well.

3. **In no more** than one sentence, write what you stand for. What's your "mission" as the boss? If you don't know this or can't articulate it, then you're going to be like the dog owner who confuses his pet with alternating messages and commands. Think about why you took this job. Or consider what you'd like to hear will be said about your contribution after you're gone.

Communication

WEEK TWO | MEETINGS

People who like meetings enjoy them for a lot of different reasons. Some, believe it or not, actually enjoy getting something accomplished. Others, like a longtime friend of mine, just like getting off their feet and away from the public for a while. This librarian would challenge himself (and the rest of us, if we dared) to "filibuster" the boss on a key question or two at the end of the meeting, just to see how long he could extend his "reprieve" from the public service desk. The best meetings I knew of were run by a company owner who had painted a basketball court in his warehouse and held meetings "in the paint," with no chairs. Staff would gather standing round the mike, announcements were made, awards or concerns distributed, and then everyone went back to work.

In all the years I've been running meetings, I've tried to find a common ground between each of those elements—giving staff some breathing room, accomplishing something, but not wasting anyone's time. It isn't easy. A few guidelines have emerged over the years, though, and good bosses need to consider them and continually strive to make their meetings a good source of communication with staff, rather than just a time-wasting placeholder.

Have an agenda or don't have the meeting. Agendas make meetings productive. Without them, human nature takes over and groups end up commiserating (or whining, at their worst), running around in verbal circles, and ultimately going nowhere. And don't just create an agenda on the back of an envelope five minutes before the meeting starts. A week to a few days before your meeting, take time to think creatively about what you're going to be there to accomplish. If you find yourself staring at a blank piece of (virtual) paper and nothing's coming to you, then cancel the meeting. Nobody, and I mean nobody, wants to sit through a purposeless meeting. Sending your agenda out ahead of time will also give staff a precious opportunity to gather their thoughts, or review materials, and make more valuable contributions to the discussion.

FOR EVERY POTENTIAL MEETING PITFALL, THERE IS a SOLUTION

HURTS THE MEETING	HELPS THE MEETING
Unclear purpose	An agenda defines why you are there.
Uneven participation	Share facilitation and training roles.
Straying off task	Create a timed agenda and stick to it. If a discussion goes over the time limit, "park it" for further review and discussion and a later decision.
No decision made	Have key decision-makers in place, and a goal established.
No follow-up	Once decided, do it. Don't let meeting results be ignored.[3]

Direct it, don't star in it. One boss I had never spoke a single word at her meetings, other than to introduce each new topic. She was there to listen and learn from her staff. If you have "team" meetings, share the facilitation duties between everyone. You'll also be helping them to build those ever-important communication skills. By sharing meeting leadership, not only will you end up hearing from more people, but you'll convince your staff that they too are truly important members of the group. Even if some may seem reluctant at first to "lead," you can convince them that everyone will benefit as the team hears a fresh approach, grows more invested, and builds leadership within the staff.

Capitalize on the opportunity to develop your team. Imagine how fortunate you are at a meeting of department heads or managers to have gathered together all of those combined years of experience, knowledge, and creativity at one table. Don't waste it. Use every single meeting as a growth opportunity as well. Divide every agenda in half (if you can) and keep the business part short so the other portion can be learning. You're not going to have to spend money on speakers or trainers to fill that time. First, if you don't already have a model for shared learning in place, this is a good time to add one. Every time someone on your staff attends an outside workshop or conference, put them on the next meeting's agenda to share what they learned. Also, remember that what's good for our customers (book discussions) can be good for our staff members as well. Find a development, management, or motivational title that matches your staff needs and buy everyone a copy (paperbacks online are cheap), then use it as an ongoing discussion topic over a series of meetings. Recently, our management team read *Ideas Are Free* by Alan Robinson and Dean Schroeder, and as a result, each of their department meetings now begins with collection-great, service-focused, and money-saving ideas from their staffs.

Meet vertically. Way too often, groups or teams of people will be formed from a horizontal section of your library, creating a tainted, almost stereotypic vision of library operations. Think about it. Managers' meetings are all people in at least basic supervisory roles or above. Collection development team meetings are usually all librarians, at least. What about all the other views of our library that we're missing? Your meetings should include them, if not through actual, permanent membership in the group, then at least by making others into "guest speakers." If, for example, the library's collection development team was broadened to include someone from technical services, plus some pages and staff from circulation, then collection management discussions could broaden to include critical issues such as time for processing or delivering and what's *really* on the minds of your customers (no one knows that like circulation staff).

Finally, meet like you mean it. Rushing in from a meeting at headquarters, the manager was already late for her building's staff meeting. Everyone from pages to librarians to specialists had already been assembled in the meeting room for twenty minutes when they heard her car screech around the corner and come to a screaming halt in her spot just outside the door. Papers flying, she rushed into the room, dropped her notebooks and binders in a heap next to her chair, whispered something to her patient assistant sitting beside her, and dove right in. "Okay, we've got a couple of major problems to discuss today and I want some answers to what happened during that incident last week, so let's get started." She glanced quickly at her watch. "I don't have much time." True story.

What's wrong with this scenario? Plenty, if you want to be a *great* boss. First of all, why even call a meeting when you obviously don't have time for one? Second, how about a brief "Nice to see all of you. Thanks for your hard work" beginning? Would it have killed her to try a little "appreciative leadership" at the opening of this meeting? I think not. And finally, how important could *any* of what they were going to discuss there be when, obviously, the entire meeting was just shoehorned into the day? If you don't *really* have something to say to your staff and you don't *really* want to hear what they'll say back, and you don't *really* have the time to meet, then don't meet. Send out a memo, or, better yet, your assistant, to gather the info you need and let everyone stay at their post. At least then, their time would be better appreciated.

Suggested Reading

Robinson, Alan G., and Dean M. Schroeder. *Ideas Are Free: How the Idea Revolution Is Liberating People and Transforming Organizations.* San Francisco: Berrett-Koehler, 2004.

WORKSHEET

1. **You have a** file for the meetings you run, right? If so, review your meeting agendas and minutes for the past six months. Did all your "to-do" notes in the margins get done? If not, maybe you need a new follow-up system. What steps could you add to be *sure* your purposeful meetings result in action? Jot some ideas below.

2. **Back to question** 1: if you don't have that file, then start one now. After each meeting, you should be clipping your agenda to the minutes and transferring the action steps to a log or calendar you monitor daily, until each item is checked off. The time it takes to set up this type of organization pays off in ways you couldn't even imagine. Set that system up now.

3. **How do you** make meetings fun and worthwhile? List as many ideas as you can think of to jazz up your next meeting. Can you feature a staff speaker? Can someone share jewels from a recent training? Have you read an article lately you'd like to share or discuss? Can you bring in a community leader or business partner to talk about the future?

4. **Create your next** meeting's agenda now. After writing it, check to see if there are topics you can handle in other ways, such as small group meetings or even just in e-mail. If you can, replace them with some of your ideas from question 3.

5. **Finally, list the** staff members who attend your meetings and, next to each name, write a month of the year. Now, when preparing agendas for those upcoming meetings, contact that person and negotiate a way to involve them in the leadership or learning that will take place.

Communication

WEEK THREE | WRITING

In writing, short is best. That could have been said another way. Usually, when you're trying to convey something in writing, whether through an article or a letter or even by e-mail, it's best to be sure that you say as much as you can with as few words as possible, so as to have the most profound impact on the reader. Now please reread the first sentence. See what I mean?

In my first year of journalism school at Kent State University, I had a wonderful "Reporting 101" teacher. She was actually a real live reporter who had decided to take a year off and try teaching. Here's the best assignment she gave us, which I've never forgotten. She first passed out a fact sheet that contained, in random order, dozens of pieces of information. We were to read them over quickly. They included items such as

> Freeway; car accident; drunk driver; three dogs; circus van; driver decapitated; baby run over; State Route 271; Monday, July 20; car explosion; Siamese twins injured; 6:30 p.m.; priest paralyzed; slippery roads; no insurance; fourth offense; radio audible (rock 'n roll) through sirens; beer cans strewn across median; rescue helicopter crashes; "can't see through smoke."

Dazed and confused (and freshmen), we followed her next instruction and wrote a ten-column-inch news story out of all that. It was hard to sort through and find any part of the story we could exclude, especially with that space limitation. Oh, yes, we also had only fifteen minutes in which to write it. Then, when we put down our pens, she announced, "Nuclear weapons have just been fired at the United States. The city editor needs more space. Cut your story to five column inches—and make it good!"

In writing, short *is* best. Most of what we write could easily be cut in half and still be as effective or even made more so. That's why one of the first and most important rules of writing is to *have an editor.* As the boss, you'll be expected to do a lot of writing. And if you've been the boss for a while and you haven't done much writing, then you've missed out on a great opportunity. Whether penning an editorial for the local newspaper, a report for the board, or an e-mail to the staff, make sure you say what you want to say, make it interesting, keep it brief, and have someone look it over first.

Another important writing tip to remember as the boss is that you should assume that every single thing you write might someday be handed to you, in court, while you're in the witness stand, by an opposing attorney who then inquires, "You wrote this. Did you not?" Make sure you're proud of and can defend *everything* you write. Once, while on "the stand" in a labor arbitration hearing, the opposing attorney actually did pull from his briefcase a sheaf of papers about one inch thick and say to me "These are e-mails you wrote to the defendant as her supervisor. I'm going to ask you a few questions about them." Three hours' worth of a "few questions" followed. Throughout that ordeal, I alternately prayed (under my breath) that I hadn't written anything stupid or mean in a moment of frustration and thanked (also under my breath) those who had coached and trained me to "write professionally and always for public reading."

When e-mail was new and dinosaurs roamed the earth, we'd often hear the adage that before hitting "Send" (or worse, "Reply to All"), we should assume the e-mail we'd just written might make its way to be read by our mother, our worst enemy, and our minister. Now that gives new meaning to the word *reread*. But it's true. And aside from the potential legal and professional damage that a poorly written document can cause, there's also the hurt to a real person that can result. How many gossipy, exaggerated, and even contrived messages have you read that you knew, if made public, could ruin someone or cause them great pain?

So, having said all this, what are the rules for good writing? Hmmm. Somerset Maugham answered this for us once when he said: "There are three rules for the writing of a novel. Unfortunately, no one knows what they are."[4]

But what's the best, the very best advice a writer can get? It is to be yourself. Often, someone will ask, "Will you listen to this and tell me what you think?" Then they'll read a passage they've just written and you are stuck trying to find a nice way to say it's stilted or too stuffy or even theatrical. Many writers, especially amateurs, think the longer the sentence and the more flowery the words, the better the writing. You've probably heard the adage, "Write what you know." Well, to that you might add, "Write like you speak." Be yourself. Read what you've written out loud and listen to it. Does it sound real? Does it sound like you? I often ask writers, "If you weren't writing it but were just saying it, how would you say it? Then write it that way."

Eudora Welty *heard* her pages speak. She explained once that "ever since I was first read to, then started reading to myself, there has never been a line read that I didn't *hear* . . . My own words, when I am at work on a story, I hear too as they go, in the same voice that I hear when I read in books . . . I have always trusted this voice."[5]

You are the boss because of who you are. So don't try to write, act, or speak like someone else. Trust in yourself and others will do the same.

WORKSHEET

1. **You knew this** was coming. Using the facts below (and making up what you have to in order to tie it together), write a brief story for your internal staff newsletter. (Plotline hint: things looked terrible, but then lots happened and things got better.)

Twenty-three layoffs, reduced health benefits, history of library funding for past ten years, legislative arguing, two-year budget, recession, collection development reductions, phasing out of videocassettes, hiring freeze, lobbyists, e-mail and petition drive, trustees traveling to state capital, no pay raise, voluntary furloughs, customer service, closed on Saturdays, windfall donation, extended hours, more library staff, expanding outreach department, building a new branch.

2. **Reread your article** or, if you're brave, ask a colleague to read it for you and answer these questions: Was it dry? Was it interesting? Did it keep her attention? Was it clear or rambling? Now rewrite it below, correcting everything that you can and making it only half as long.

3. **Pull out the** last several things you've written in your job and do the same for them. Whether they are e-mails or reports or a newspaper column, think about how they could be better. What aspects of your writing could you improve, and how, exactly, do you plan to do so?

Communication

WEEK FOUR | WHAT NOT TO SAY

No. Let's start with that. When considering things that good bosses should *never* say, the word *no* comes immediately to mind. But that doesn't mean that you should agree with everything. What it does mean is that you should approach all of your communication, written, oral, and implied, with a positive attitude. You and your communication style will set the tone for your library. You will establish, whether you want to or not, the "reputation" your library has among other librarians, with the community, and (please don't forget this) with your director or the board. So, should you ever be negative or snide or flip in your communication? Perhaps there is another way to be. (Notice, I didn't say "no" but I meant it.)

Consider the questions you ask. Are you asking the right thing or the wrong thing? As the boss, you need to be accountable. One manager told me that as soon as you take on *any* position of responsibility, then every problem you see or hear about is yours. You must be accountable for either solving it or seeing to it that it gets into the hands of someone who can. No more whining or hand-wringing or complaining. You're the boss now.

In one of the most persuasive books I've ever read on personal and professional accountability, author John Miller clarifies that we can be "making better choices in the moment by asking better questions."[6] It's simple since, in his view, all we have to do is *not* say a few words and make sure our questions follow three simple rules. First, do *not* begin a question with *why, when,* or *who.* Rather, always begin a question with *what* or *how.* Next, make sure your questions contain *I* instead of *they, them, we,* or *you.* And finally, make sure your questions focus on *action.*

Many would suggest that the secret to positive communication isn't in *what* you say, but in *how* you say it. In one particularly useful workshop about how to have a difficult conversation, the speaker suggested that you should always begin by stating, "You and I are about to have a very difficult conversation." Set the

Miller suggests that if you consider what is being communicated by these questions and then by the QBQ, or the "question behind the question," you can avoid any further victim thinking, procrastinating, or blaming; you can realize that you can only change you and, most important, you can take action.

YOUR QUESTION	**QBQ**
Why don't others work harder?	How can I do my job better today?
Why is this happening to me?	What can I do to improve the situation?
Why do they make it so difficult for me to do my job?	How can I support others?
When will they take care of the problem?	What solution can I provide?
When will we get the information we need to make a decision?	What can I do to find the information to make a decision?[7]

tone honestly from the very beginning. This will help give you the courage you need (and, yes, you need to be courageous sometimes) to say things like "One of your coworkers has charged that you touched her inappropriately" or something equally as sensitive. It's always hardest to have to discipline an otherwise excellent employee, such as the librarian with the very best customer service skills, who is always late for work. Setting the "this will be difficult" stage early on will help buy you time to make your case fairly and thoroughly.

Another helpful maneuver is to always give people an "out," even if they don't deserve it. This nonthreatening approach usually begins with "You may not be aware of this, but . . ." I've used this effective entrance with everyone from staff stalkers to inattentive mothers and sex surfers. You're not doing the offender any favors when you give him a graceful way to stop the inappropriate behavior because, in the end, you're still getting him to stop the inappropriate behavior. It's one of those rare instances where everyone, including all other library staff and customers, can win. This approach can work with that tardy employee too. "You may not be aware of this, but you are considered a leader on our reference team and coming in late every day is having a really negative effect on the staff."

Above all else, *say something*. You are the boss. Remember, as the boss, you own every problem. Until you either fix it or hand it over to someone else who can, say something, do something, decide something. Be part of the solution, not part of the problem.

Suggested Reading

Miller, John G. *QBQ! The Question behind the Question: What to Really Ask Yourself to Eliminate Blame, Complaining and Procrastination. Practicing Personal Accountability at Work and in Life.* New York: G. P. Putnam's Sons, 2004.

WORKSHEET

16

For each section, use a real-life situation going on in your library today. Fill in a question, using the first word provided, that you might ask if you were shirking your responsibilities as a boss.

Then rewrite the question using the "QBQ" method to demonstrate how you could assume accountability for the problem.

1. **Why are/is** ______________________________

    (Focus on action.) **What/How** can I ______________________________

2. **When will** ______________________________

    (Focus on action.) **What/How** can I ______________________________

3. **Who will** ______________________________

    (Focus on action.) **What/How** can I ______________________________

4. **What one thing** (if you're normal, there are probably many from which to select) did you most recently communicate that was negative? Something that you wish you had *not* said or had said differently? How might you have communicated it better?

Customer Service

WEEK ONE | THE PEOPLE

On their first day at work, new reference staff members in my old library used to be scared to death. Surrounded by literally hundreds of specialized fine-arts reference titles, professionals and paraprofessionals alike feared their inexperience and lack of knowledge would be a disappointment to both our customers and coworkers. There was just *so* much to learn, they'd tell me, they'll never do it!

No, there wasn't so much to learn. On dozens of those "first mornings," I'd explain to them that there was only *one* thing they needed to learn and to do in order to be a complete success on the job and a benefit to our library. There was only one thing I would ask of them, and they already knew how to do it. Just be kind to people. All people. The customers they encountered and the staff with whom they worked side by side. I'd assure them that if they helped each customer with a smile and made sure that customer left our library wanting to come back, then they were already a success on the job. All the other "stuff" they'd learn eventually would just be icing on the cake.

Customer service is staff.

Everything else is just window dressing.

Some of you are new to libraries, as well as to being the boss. Let me share a historical tidbit with you. For many years, you can find professional journal articles in which we have continually bemoaned our "reputation" as unfair. We're caricatured as stuffy, bossy, critical, and "tight-bunned." But in truth, we were. While we all, as the Three Stooges used to say, "resembled that remark," it was actually pretty accurate. And there was only one way to change it, and that was to change ourselves. That's why improving customer service now is so easy, at least to get started. All we have to do is be nice(r). A renowned national specialist on this topic, Joan Frye Williams, offers this advice for our libraries. "Be more pleasant to people. Make the atmosphere not so clinical. Relax a bit on the restrictions. Lighten up. Stop making it feel so much like church."[1]

William Schroer, in a presentation entitled "Customer Service or . . . Customer Servant? Delivering Excellent Customer Service without Giving Up or Giving In," calls your staff member's one chance to make a positive impression the "moment of truth."

This is the moment when your library has the golden opportunity to make the experience worth repeating (meaning the customer comes back) or not.

Managing the Moments of Truth

- Be welcoming, as though each customer is a guest in your home
- Be helpful
- Be engaging
- Introduce yourself—use your name
- Learn your customer's name
- Be a partner in the solution they seek; don't just point and sit back down
- Follow up, remembering their name (you wrote it down)[2]

Steve Wishnack suggests your staff members have three opportunities to make a good impression on your customers.

1. When they first connect
2. When they contribute to meeting needs
3. At the end, when they say "thanks"

If staff succeed, you'll have a loyal customer for life. If they fail or show they don't care enough, your library is in trouble.[5]

In short, we had *earned* our reputation (most reputations are deserved). The public saw us and our libraries through the lens *we had created!* But today it's time to be all about our customers, not all about our rules. Williams and copresenter George Needham also agree that in order to thrive, our service models need to adapt to today and be more about experience. We need to be "more self-directed and have less waiting, consider reducing or eliminating fines and provide 'zone staffing' (so there's always someone there when you need them)."[3] It is time to stop thinking of ourselves as gatekeepers to the information world and transition to being guides. We need to be nicer. To share. To make our customers feel more comfortable. Like I said, we just need to become more kind. Somewhere in the past twenty years, we started calling that "customer service."

Starting with the thesis that "every patron is important, but some are very special," libraries need to establish a very basic, agreed-upon philosophy on which they can then build more modern customer experiences.[4] But you need to be sure your staff aren't just paying lip service to that philosophy. They have to think that and feel it and believe it and show it in all they do. As the boss, new or old, you might find this simple but critical step daunting. How can you possibly train and motivate staff to do this? It's really a lot simpler than it sounds.

The secret is to not get off track with staff. Especially when orienting new staff, don't even begin to veer off into operational issues such as collections or programs or even specific reference tools until this underlying theme of how to treat people is established. It's simple. Keep it simple for your staff. Stay focused on the customer at all times.

"Customer needs begin with the need to be safe and secure. Add to that the need to be liked, listened to, acknowledged, appreciated and understood. There's also the need to trust and be trusted, accepted, respected, valued and connected to other people . . . Ultimately, what matters *most* to customers is how they are treated."[6]

If you can get your staff to believe in these guidelines, then you've all mastered customer service. Now you can start working on the window dressing.

One final note about your staff and their role in your customer service success. With all your encouragement and modeling and coaching and training, nothing will work unless the customer and the staff member interact at the point of need. Today's library literature is full of pleas to get staff out from behind their desks. It's been called intercepting or hip-to-hip service or roving reference. Early in my career, we used to call it pointing with our feet, not our hands. Whatever you call it, it's the undeniable wave of the future success of libraries to stop acting like the king of the world, ensconced comfortably behind a huge wooden barrier, too busy (or at least looking that way) to be bothered with the queries of the peons. Stand up, care about people, be out on the floor, and build customer loyalty. The alternatives are dire. George Needham once referred to a list of things that are predicted to be extinct by 2019—less than ten years from now. It included mending clothes, getting lost, retirement, blogging, keys, coins, and, yes, you guessed it, "libraries."[7]

We can change that.

WORKSHEET

1. **Everyone has one** place (at least) where they received such poor service that they swore they'd never return. Think of yours and list at least ten feelings or impressions you had about the treatment you received.

2. **Do the same** thing as in the previous question, but this time do it for the one place you most enjoy visiting. What are at least ten reasons you like being there?

3. **Go outside right** now. Take with you Schroer's list of how to manage the "moment of truth." Follow (discreetly) one customer around and take notes on how many of these factors she experienced. Then come back to your desk and start listing what you need to do about it.

Customer Service

WEEK TWO | THE PLACE

"Feast your eyes. It's big and beige and boxy. Virtually featureless. What else could it be? We're here."[8] While Paco Underhill's less than enthusiastic description is actually of a shopping mall, he could just as easily be talking about one of the thousands of libraries scattered around the country. Unless you're lucky enough to be working in something recently featured in a library architecture journal, you're more than likely spending your days in an age-old, built-with-public-money structure that has little more to offer visitors than limited parking and confusing hours. We can learn a lot from making the comparison between our libraries and a shopping mall. Consider the parallel, for example, between both of our front doors.

"Anyway, here we are. What do we see? 'A big wall with a little mouse hole?'"[9] Most good customer service reviews need to begin not inside our buildings or even with our collections but on the outside, taking our buildings, grounds, access, hours, and even phone directory ads into consideration. Even if we assume our customers can find our address, get to our libraries, arrive when we're open (what's with all these openings and closings on the half hour, anyway? Do they just make scheduling around lunch hours easier for *us*?), park, and get inside, what then? How, in the jumble of rooms that we've decided represent departments, can they ever begin to find their way? And God help them if they don't speak English.

We'll never make it work for them until we start thinking like they do. And we don't have to invent this method ourselves. In a book about the spectacular customer service success of Nordstrom department stores, authors Spector and McCarthy put it simply. "Nordstrom is a company whose managers constantly reinforce . . . its unwavering dedication to *think like the customer*. This is the essence of a great customer-service company."[10]

Let's be honest. Libraries before the 1980s or so could not even come close to claiming that intention. Where did we put our most popular reference books? Near the front door where they were easy to access? Hardly. Try in the back of the second floor, in the lower desk of the librarian who required a photo ID and

Williams uses our buildings' customer service features to differentiate between libraries you wouldn't revisit and those you would.

Pass/Fail? These Fail!

- Libraries with inhospitable surroundings
- Lack of parking
- Buildings showing dirt, wear, shabbiness
- Inconvenient hours

Destination Libraries!

- Warm welcome
- Clean and comfortable
- Good transit options or parking
- Natural light
- Beautiful views
- "Stay a While" (comfortable) seating
- Landmark/civic pride[11]

tissue sample in order to retrieve them. When families began working multiple part-time jobs and, therefore, were unable to access our services during our "normal" business hours, did most of us decide to stay open until 10:00 or 11:00 p.m.? What about Sundays during the (gasp!) summer? Not for our staffs! And finally, consider this. What do you think happened most frequently to messy restrooms after, say, 7:00 p.m.? Were they quickly spruced up for the late evening rush or left for the morning maintenance crew? I personally had to hang up a lot of "Out of Order" signs that would remain there for the entire *weekend,* because there was no available maintenance crew.

National library expert Joan Frye Williams puts more than just personal experience behind her agreement with these issues. She quotes everything from "community assessments, strategic planning data, town meetings, user surveys, focus groups, interviews and nosiness" to back up these claims.[12] She refers to customers as *civilians* and tells us, in so many words, they've had it!

It's time to clean up our act. No amount of fabulous interpersonal service will help our libraries survive if we can't even get people in the door. You're the boss now, so just as your home reflects on you, the condition and appearance of your facility also show how important you think your customers are. No money? Organize some volunteers. Many libraries work successfully with their local gardening clubs to keep their grounds looking beautiful. Others opt for the "freeway" approach of asking families to "adopt" a flower bed, and then they prominently display a thank-you sign in the bed to both acknowledge their community's investment and to encourage similar volunteers.

Painting is cheap. Usually, you can buy it with pizza. If you don't already have an active youth volunteer or Friends group, start one. Get a couple of interested parents to help supervise and you can freshen up a room with just an extra-large pizza with anchovies. Don't worry about mistakes or the occasional drip on the carpet. Inarguably, the place will look better—overall—when you're done than when you started. Another successful venture can be to plan a summer "Teen Library Camp," where the kids complete a different service project for you each week. In return, you'll be providing them with a valuable mock-employment experience and, in the end, you both will win.

Aesthetics matter to everyone, young and old. Most of us don't have the money to undertake major renovations, but you can still think of both your customers and your staff members and make minor changes that will demonstrate how much you care about their enjoyment of the library. Go outside and look in your windows. What do you see? If all you see is books, then you're wasting both the view and natural sunlight on a bunch of dusty, inanimate objects. Move the shelves back and put some furniture near the window. If you can't afford to buy it, ask a local furniture store to "loan" you some discontinued pieces and advertise for them with a "thank you to . . ." note near the seating. And when it comes to comfort and aesthetics, please don't forget your staff.

Make sure their staff room is bright, warm, and comfortable. Your "internal customers" also need to feel valued, and anything you can do to enhance the many hours they spend under your roof will come back to benefit you all in ways you can't even imagine.

Suggested Reading

Underhill, Paco. *Call of the Mall.* New York: Simon and Schuster, 2004.

WORKSHEET

1. **Take this workbook** and walk around the outside of your library, making notes below as you go. Note whether each area needs improvement and start thinking about how you might start making some positive changes.

   Parking __________
   Building condition __________
   Accessible __________
   Entrances inviting __________
   Hours visible and convenient __________
   Other impressions __________

2. **Now go inside,** through the front door. Keep making notes about the customer service "feel" of your building and how it might be improved.

   Directional signs friendly and helpful __________
   Staff available to greet __________
   Staff offering help __________
   No deluge of "don't do this or that" signage __________
   Interior attractiveness __________
   Comfortable seating available __________
   Conduct under control __________
   Staff acting professionally __________
   Good lighting available __________
   Other impressions __________

3. **Next, get out** your local yellow pages (or log on to them, if you prefer) and start a list right now of companies that might be interested in lending a hand. Most small businesses have a very limited budget for advertising, but you can offer them *free* marketing to the thousands of your shared customers who walk through your doors each year.

   Gardening __________
   Furniture __________
   Lighting __________
   Paint/decorating __________
   Other ideas __________

4. **Finally, if you** don't already have a volunteer program going, start researching right now in library literature how you might start one. You can start small (as you can do for any change). Maybe just advertise for one "Gardening Volunteer" or one "Painting Volunteer" and go on from there. Where might you get started? If you can't find any articles to help you, e-mail me. I'd be happy to share information on my library's success.

____

____

____

____

Customer Service

WEEK THREE | VIRTUAL SERVICE

In the beginning there was a bright green, blinking light in the lower left-hand corner of the computer screen. We didn't know exactly what to do with it. The usefulness of this new technology was entirely dependent on our mastery of a series of long, complex command sequences, and our customers' benefit from the technology was negligible at worst and delayed at best. Today we're all surfing the World Wide Web, but at most libraries we still don't know what to do with it.

From the day when the first PC was brought into the library and plopped on an ergonomically inappropriate surface, we've wavered between calling it everything from a marketing tool to a reference tool, and along the journey of our indecision we've put a wide array of people in charge of it, from undertrained librarians to overskilled computer geeks. You're the boss now. What are you going to do with this virtual minefield?

If you believe, as I do, that we are truly in an *experience economy* these days, which means we have to consider *all* aspects of a library visit as critical (even electronic ones), then you might want to consider this advice from B. Joseph Pine II. According to Pine, "there are four basic kinds of experiences—entertaining, educational, escapist and aesthetic—but the *best* ones actually encompass aspects of all four."[13]

So ironically, libraries have had the Web figured out right all these years, since we've tried to match all of those things. Our library's web page *is* a marketing tool, a reference tool, and an interactive way to network with customers. But we've still missed an important point. That is, our virtual libraries *cannot* be just one of those things at a time and cannot rely on just one or two staff members to make them successful.

Today, the virtual world for which you are responsible is way too important for you not to grasp it clearly and manage it appropriately. Innovation expert Stephen

Innovation guru Stephen Abram allows us one day for rest . . . as long as we use the other six to implement what he considers to be key elements in the success of our virtual libraries:

- *Keep it personal.* Make sure your web page is marked with your library and staff's identity.
- *Blog.* These are just a series of quality conversations.
- *Tag.* This allows both description and sharing—to better serve information needs.
- *Wiki.* Share and organize huge amounts of info. Just think of Wikipedia.
- *Instant message.* A ten-minute learning curve to hit a major market.
- *Virtual reference.* Use everything to enhance this experience—info, pictures, video . . . the works.[14]

Abram puts it this way: "We are entering an era when usage of our virtual branches is outpacing our physical branches. That's not bad—both serve different clientele and program purposes. Adapting to these environments will take a high level of experimentation, consultation and collaboration, and all of this *must* occur in teams and between teams across our organizations."[15]

There's no shortage of articles, books, classes, workshops, and "experts" out there to give bosses more ideas than hours in the day about how to handle a virtual branch. Even Abram suggests one element for each day, allowing for one day of rest.

At the risk of sounding heretical, though, and even after considering all of these examples, I would suggest that the virtual world you run requires *no* different skills from those you already have. You just have to remember to use your virtual library to serve your customer—and not yourselves. After you get done loading every single set of minutes and agendas from your board meetings on your page, but before you congratulate yourselves, ask, "Do we have any customers who will care about this? Or would they rather see a timely link that changes every single morning, pointing them to books and other materials about the celebrity who just passed away, or the upcoming election, or the Olympics, or whatever?" In other words, consider the customer when asking for whom you are building these pages.

You also need to have the right people on your "virtual" bus, just as you do at other posts around the library. Don't make the mistake of hiring people who are either too technical or too librarianesque. Unlike the 1980s and '90s, when finding a trained librarian who understood technology was tantamount to finding a car mechanic who knew Dewey, today that work is—and should be—part of *everyone's* job. And so you, to be a good boss, must build the Web into every single job. Your HR person should have a "Jobs" web page that he manages on his own. Your PR person should have a "Library News" page that she can update. Long gone is the luxury of having a "web person" in the basement or somewhere who could be treated like a giant in-box of web page work. Now we all have to be able to join in or we're (excuse this overused analogy) missing the bus entirely.

Your library's web presence must be different from other web pages out on the Internet and must convey the *value* of your local library, or it isn't worth the air it's printed on. You are local. Be local. Don't worry so much about making the U.S. Constitution available to everyone at 3:00 a.m.; we all have Google for that. Worry, instead, about making the pictures of your city hall being built a hundred years ago available. Or worry about how to post the recorded local history of some of your senior citizens and their families. Where else should they look but to their library for that type of experience?

And finally, invite your customers to be part of the library's web team. Today, it's more valuable to allow customers to build their own databases of books they've read and to comment or critique as reviewers than it is to limit them to entering their own holds or renewing their own books. Open the library's web pages up to them. Ask them for family pictures and provide a scanner so they can build their own digital history. Record audio of your seniors telling war stories, or record videos of your tots at story hour. Imagine the thrill of being able to direct grandparents across the country to a YouTube segment of their own grandchildren!

We sometimes call the library's web presence our "virtual branch." Make it so. Don't treat it like a piece of marketing stationery or like a space station, which only physicists can enter. Today, the Web is an integral part of everyone's life and it should be an integral part of your library. You're the boss. Make it so!

Suggested Reading

Pine, B. Joseph, II, and James H. Gilmore. *The Experience Economy: Work Is Theatre and Every Business a Stage.* Watertown, MA: Harvard Business School Press, 1999.

WORKSHEET

1. **Go to your** library's web page and make a list of what you see there, and then note what "service" each piece represents. Think broadly and include areas such as marketing, PR, advertising, reference, programming, and so on.

2. **On a scale** of 1 to 10, be critical and "grade" each item in the list above. How successful is each aspect of your page? For everything you give a 9 or under, make some notes on either how it could be more effective or whom you could speak to about making it more effective (not everything is within your area of expertise, remember).

3. **Make a list** of all of the people who contribute to your website. On a scale of 1 to 10, how well trained and comfortable are they with these assignments? Can you help them be better? How?

4. **Thinking of the** rest of your staff, whom else might you involve in this "branch"? List their names and their potential contributions. Now, how will you go about involving them? Do you have a "web team" already? If not, maybe you should have.

5. **In preparation for** making all of these improvements, draft a "web strategic plan" for your library. Use either your web team or the staff involved to refine it, and then everyone can get to work with shared goals in mind.

Customer Service

WEEK FOUR | BABY STEPS

Someone once said that prior to the mid-1980s libraries changed at the speed of a glacier. Then, all of a sudden, everything hit at once. How can you, as the boss, get your staff successfully from your grandmother's library to the library of the twenty-first century? The answer is, you all take baby steps.

One thing is for sure, leadership through a time of this much change is not about who can yell the loudest. It's about who can speak the most clearly, make the most sense, and therefore bring the most people along with them. Imagine a staff meeting where the boss steps up to the podium and announces: "Starting tomorrow, we're going to do everything different around here. All of you who were drawn to library work because you like things in order and neat, pay attention. We're going to let customers shelve for us or just leave everything lying around. And, oh, by the way, we're also going to forget those complicated Library of Congress headings, and customers will now be allowed to create our new catalog records. We'll call them 'tags.'

"Furthermore, all of you who were drawn to this work because you're on the shy side and you're more comfortable dealing with books than people, listen up. Thanks for the last twenty years or so of your life, but get ready, starting tomorrow you're going to have to walk all around out on the floor and be outgoing and smile and greet everyone you see and initiate conversations. There's more to announce and more changes coming, but let's take a short break. Oh, by the way, there will be no more donuts at staff meetings. Please help yourself to the tofu bagels and caffeine-free weak tea. Be back in 10."

Ick. I sure don't want to work there. But wait, I think I do! I think we all do.

So what's the answer? It's not as hard as it sounds. Go slowly. Listen to the experts. Make small changes carefully and bring your staff along with you. If you make sure they know what you're asking them to do and why, eventually all of your small changes will add up and you'll have a transformed library. Let's look at how you might attack this using the "people, place, and virtual world" approach.

People. Always tell your staff *why*. For every change you make, start by addressing the need for the change, the justification, and the expected result. Make their part clear. Do they have anything to say about the changes? If so, then let them talk and listen. If not (and sometimes they won't), then tell them that honestly too. What are they supposed to say to customers who might not understand what's going on? Should everyone be saying the same thing? (Yes.) If so, then help them understand what to say and give them the language to use to help them be clear.

One library went over to self-checkout too quickly and never explained to staff why they were spending the money to do so. When customers began to ask, they got a range of responses from "I have no idea, this is just one of the boss's new kicks" to "Don't ask me, I just work here." Another library boss took the time to show everyone WIIFM (what's in it for me), how their workload would be positively impacted, how there would be more time for other, more interesting work and how, down the road, they wouldn't suffer from an increase in work as the budget became too tight to add staff. Their customers heard everything from "These are great time savers and they're easy to use" to "This is just one more way we're trying to protect and stretch the tax dollars we get." Which boss would you rather be?

Similarly, libraries eager to transition to the proactive service model, which gets staff out from behind their desks, have often made the mistake of presenting this change as an "all or nothing" directive that allows no chance for long-term staffers to adjust. At the King County (Washington) Library System, the recognition that time was needed to find a new level of comfort caused them to move more slowly. "We modified our goals by asking staff to rove, at a minimum, for a total of fifteen to twenty minutes during a one-hour shift," explain the reference services coordinator, Barbara Pitney, and the former assistant managing librarian, Nancy Slote.[16]

No change can succeed without the support of the people who work with it, and no support can be won without the right leadership from the boss.

Place. What about when you change the building itself or something inside it? Most of us flip through the annual architectural library miracles issues of our journals with our mouths watering. But who has an extra $20 million lying around? Here's a secret you'll be glad to know: you don't need a lot of money to "modernize" your library. There are literally hundreds of free or low-cost *baby steps* you can take to begin to

"BABY STEP IMPROVEMENTS"

People

- Smile and welcome everyone
- Get out from behind the desks
- Wear name tags, or badges with your name
- Wear a button or lanyard that says "Please Interrupt Me" or "May I Help You?"
- Ask permission before placing someone on hold
- Use volunteers to act as greeters
- Make generic business cards for *all* staff with their name, URL for library, and phone number
- Find out what your staff are involved or interested in out in the community and support them as ambassadors of your library
- Take appointments
- Train all staff to deal with youth
- Show enthusiasm!

Place

- Make frequent changes to the building's exterior (balloons, banners, signs)
- Make sure all signs have positive messages
  - Do Not Enter until 9:00 — No!
  - It's Almost Time, We Open at 9:00 — Yes!
- Rearrange furniture to face windows
- Add footstools
- Designate at least one "Quiet Zone"
- Allow food and drink
- Post a "Today" sign near your entrance

Virtual Library

- Put *everything* local that you can find on your web page
- Post a relevant library connection to the day's news and update it daily
- Allow customers to add content (reviews, etc.)
- Link to and with everyone in your community
- Post an "Internet Tip of the Week"
- Experiment with instant messaging and blogs[17]

transform your old-fashioned building into something that looks like and acts like today's library.

Later, when you get to the bigger projects, do them one at a time as well. If you and your staff can prioritize the projects you most desire to accomplish, you can then go after funding and support for each one based on its own merits and benefits. For example, get as professional a drawing as possible made of the children's reading garden you'd like to add off the storytime room, then get some publicity for it. Your local newspaper is your best first bet, but if that doesn't work, then create your own oversized posters and display them on easels around your library (or in the lobby of your public schools, with permission). How much money do you need to raise? For a small amount, sell individual bricks to your customers. For a bit more, go to local merchants for support. For even more than that, get started on some funding research and see if you can land a grant.

The details may change a bit but the path is always the same for change. Start small and keep building.

Virtual world. What about on the Web? Most of us can't go out and hire someone to transform our Internet presence, nor can we miraculously retrain our staff overnight to do so. What are some options for transformation on this front? There are several, and today most of them have to do with letting your customers help with design and content on your space. Where can members of the PTA go to comment on the summer reading list? Can members of your Mystery Book Group share reviews? Don't forget the kids. Ask for teen programming ideas online, then bring them to life. Get people involved. You might even want to start a special "Web Friends" group, just to be sure your virtual branch is meeting the *real* needs of your wired community. But even on the Web, go slowly and take your renaissance one piece at a time.

Unquestionably, getting from here to there isn't easy. The monumental shift in customer service needs and expectations in today's library provides a daunting challenge, even for the most seasoned bosses. How many articles have you read or workshops have you seen that offer advice on "How to Deal with Change"? How about "Turbulent Times," or "Leading through Change"? The list goes on and on. There are a couple of factors that emerge from all the good advice out there that bosses need to hear. They're true. They're indisputable and they're critical.

First and foremost, make sure your staff can be successful, but don't take on the sole responsibility for that outcome. I've already referred to the adage that the job of a good boss is to get work out of other people. I don't know if I like the sound of that, but the underlying message rings true. You have undoubtedly, under your roof, the equivalent of dozens if not hundreds of years of library experience, knowledge, and creativity. They are your staff. Give them the direction and tools they need, and you can lead them through any change you face. And they can do it one customer at a time. A parallel to the adage, "A single duck bite won't hurt you but a thousand can kill you,"[18] might be one smile won't turn your library around, but a thousand will put—and keep—you on the map!

Secondly, communicate well. Tell staff what they're going to have to know. Then tell them what they need to know. Then tell them what you told them. Be honest, consistent, and clear, especially when it comes to *why* your library is making a change. Paint a clear picture for them of what your library service *could* be and get and keep them on board for the ride. Ask for their feedback. Then listen.

Next, don't waver. Don't change your mind based on the most recent plea you've heard. Transforming your service model and bringing your library in line with today's realities isn't going to be easy. Public librarianship in the twenty-first century is not for the faint of heart!

Finally, perhaps more than anything else, be a leader. Change, and success, require real leadership. So does your staff. The bottom line is always the customer and, as the Nordstrom team says, the desire to "outservice, not outsmart."[19]

WORKSHEET

1. PEOPLE. **Simply list,** in a stream-of-consciousness sort of way, all of the innovations you'd like to see in your library that your staff can accomplish.

2. **Using the above** list, note one small step you can help your staff take to accomplish each innovation.

3. BUILDING. **What changes** can you make for absolutely free? First, list the ones that you can think of. Then send an "all-staff" e-mail and offer to provide a pizza lunch to the department that can come up with the most useful, free suggestions for building improvements. Give them about one week to submit them. Don't forget to have fun at lunch.

4. VIRTUAL. **Log on to** your website right now. What was put up there today? What could have been put up? Did the state legislature just vote on your budget? Could you have announced that in a simple headline, and then linked to the governor's page? What else? Think back over the past seven days and list one thing that you could have posted every day, just to remind your customers that (1) you actually do keep your page current, and (2) there really are things at their library that apply to their day-to-day lives. Use this list at your web team's next meeting to get everyone else on board with this idea.

Planning

WEEK ONE | WHY PLAN?

Who can resist starting a section on strategic planning with Yogi Berra's famous comment that "if you don't know where you are going, you will wind up somewhere else"?[1] Obviously, not me.

But it's true. You want to be the best boss you can be, which means people will be depending on you to *lead*. In order to do that effectively, you have to know where you're going.

One thing I've learned clearly and indisputably as a boss is that success takes more than strategic *planning*. It takes strategic thinking and strategic management as well. But that all starts with planning, so you and your staff know where you're headed and how you're going to know when you arrive.

Strategic planning has a bad rap, in most places. Just mention that you're about to initiate a new strategic planning process and most people will roll their eyes so far back they'll pitch out of their chairs. But that's because every boss—before you—has made it boring at best and worthless at worst. It's time to change all that. Why don't you start with the jargon?

No matter how you slice it, the purpose of strategic planning is to look to the future. So don't call them "goals." Instead, call it "the future." Don't say "We're going to work now to establish our library's goals." Instead, say "Let's plan for this library's future." Simpler and clearer, I think. Next, try not to describe "strategy" as being a process of careful, measured thought that is designed to make a change and attain a certain measurable achievement—well, yawn, you see what I mean. Instead, explain that talking about "strategy" means identifying "the difference between today and tomorrow."

You'll find it's important to know what you're trying to do, what's been done before, and what options you have for the future when you're making decisions that will determine the fate of your library and staff. If that sounds a bit

Why PLAN to MOVE FORWARD?

- The riskiest proposition of all is sticking to the status quo, especially in conservative times.
- When the world around you changes, maintaining your equilibrium is a threat to your future existence.
- Fear is a strategy for the number two or number three player.[2]

PLANNING to WIN

- Let your imagination drive your vision.
- If you don't have audacious goals, your people will be status quo instead of status go.
- Make bold moves, knowing that some will work and some won't.
- Or make no move, which guarantees that you'll be an also-ran.[4]

dramatic, too bad. This is important stuff, and that environmental scan or SWOT analysis (strengths, weaknesses, opportunities, threats) is an integral part of the process. But you can make that more engaging too. Remember, good plans outline action, not escape. It's all in how you approach it. And just in case you're starting to wonder if this is all worth it, consider the alternative.

Another benefit, other than a successful library, of having a plan or a strategy in place is that it puts you in a much better position to deal with the surprises you'll inevitably face. I have to refer back to my "whitewater rafting" analogy from earlier in this book. If you're trained and dressed and practiced for those wild waves to hit you from the front, chances are you'll have more of a chance to survive than if you're still in your pajamas and you didn't think to bring the proverbial paddle. An alternative plan, of course, is to never leave the shore. But that's not really planning, it's just hiding.

Peter Schwartz, author of *Inevitable Surprises,* asked: "Is there a better way to live . . . than just to hang on for the roller-coaster ride and react to every new surprise thrust at you? Yes, there is. There are many things we can rely on, but three of them are most critical to keep in mind in any turbulent environment. First: There will be more surprises. Second: We will be able to deal with them. Third: We can anticipate [read "plan for"] many of them."[3]

So we have to plan. I hope we're agreed on that by now. In later weeks of this month, you'll learn about and consider many different ways to do that, but before you can begin using *any* method of planning, you have to start with the basics: make sure your library has clarified its *vision, values,* and *mission,* since those concepts are your guideposts along the way. Lots of people get lost between here and there (mission and completed plan), before they ever really get started. If you're leading this newest strategic planning journey, slow down a bit at this point and, as with all parts of this planning process, simplify, simplify, simplify.

National library consultant Pat Wagner suggests you use these very simple analogies to differentiate between two of the concepts (we'll talk about values later). "The *vision* is about the *better future of the people* who live, work and visit your community. Where are you going and why? The *mission* is *what the library is going to do* to make that better future happen."[5]

It's exciting to be the library in the neighborhood, the region, the state, or even in the nation that's known for leading the way. But the most valuable part of that comes when and if your customers feel the same way about what you're doing. Plan for it—and you'll probably be right. Hopefully, you'll even be surprised!

Suggested Reading

Schwartz, Peter. *Inevitable Surprises: Thinking Ahead in a Time of Turbulence.* New York: Gotham/Penguin, 2003.

WORKSHEET

1. **If things go** well, what are the three greatest things that *might* happen to your library in the next year or two?

2. **If things don't** go so well, what are the three worst things that might happen?

3. **Chart out some** ideas about how you might ensure the good things (or at least help them along) and avoid the bad things.

4. **Now, assume you** took all the work you've just done and put it in a binder, sealed it with wax, showed it to no one, and put it in a drawer. Would it be helpful? Probably not. So list how you might make it come to life *as part of a plan*. What are at least the first steps you could take to put together a planning process that would work for your library, your community, your staff, and the board?

5. **Look at your** library's existing plan. Compare it to all the ideas and creativity found just in this exercise alone. Write a justification for trying a different planning approach (this should be something you can share with your board and colleagues.) How can you improve planning in your library? And why should you?

Planning

WEEK TWO | BASIC FOUNDATIONS

This is your (and your library's) opportunity to shine. If you, as the boss, can actually lead a planning process that's exciting, challenging, and motivating and then make the results of that plan *really happen* . . . buildings will be named after you! Well, maybe not, but you'll have had a positive impact on your library's future and, after all, that's what we're all here for, right?

The good news is you *can* do all of that and it's not as difficult as you might imagine. Last week, you were (hopefully) convinced of the necessity to plan. Now, here comes the good news: planning *can* be easy. And fun. And motivating! It can be painless and it can work. Like most things, all it needs is a great leader, and that's where you come in.

Also, like most things, strategic planning models can be found on a continuum scale that runs from simple to complex and from historic to modern. I'm sure, working in a library, no one needs to tell you how many books there are on this subject, with each one apparently more tomelike and suffocating than the next. The truth is, you're probably going to have to peruse some of them at some point. You're also going to have to speak to a lot of your more experienced peers and, most likely, you're going to have to take a workshop or two. But all of these efforts will pay off a hundredfold when you see the focused efforts of your staff and the expenditures of your library's budget reaching goal after goal and truly meeting the ever-changing needs of your community.

Everyone has to start somewhere and you need to start with the basics, which involves an understanding, clarification, and reaffirmation or updating of your library's *mission, vision,* and *values.* That's the basis of everything else to come.

To get started, you'll first need to rearrange these primary concepts into an order that makes more sense. I think you should start with values, since they are clearly the foundation on which everything else rests. Then you'll move on to ask, "Where should our library be one year from now?" Or two or three . . . We'll talk more about

MISSION, VISION, and VALUES: The FOUNDATION of YOUR PLAN

Definitions

- *Mission*—a statement that answers the question, "Why does your library exist?"
- *Vision*—a clear, compelling picture of your desired future
- *Values*—enduring beliefs that affect all behavior[6]

FOCUS PLANNING on EXCELLENCE

- "Excellence must be defined locally. It results when library services match community needs, interests, and priorities.

  [That's why you have to involve so many people in the strategic planning process.]
- Excellence . . . rests more on commitment than on unlimited resources.

  [Everyone and anyone can attain it.]
- Excellence is a moving target—even when achieved, excellence must be continually maintained."[7]

the life expectancy of your plan later. That will be your vision. Your mission statement comes last and is just that, a statement about how you're going to get where you just decided you want to go.

If you're not familiar with the television show *Lost,* then this next analogy won't be as crystal clear to you, but think back to *Gilligan's Island* and you can probably make it work. You're on a desert island. You and some other library staff members landed there with everyone else from your plane or cruise ship or whatever you were on, and you're not getting rescued anytime soon. So what do you do to pass the time? You decide to build a library.

You're starting from scratch and so you ask the crowd, "What will this library stand for? What will we keep in mind as we build it? What will really matter?" Perhaps you'll hear answers like freedom, no discrimination, something for everyone, no costs, nobody tells us what we can and can't read, and so on. And there you have your values: intellectual freedom, equal access, and community literacy. This can be a very rewarding exercise to run through with your staff or the community during your planning process. What it does in the end is make people feel better about how well your library works to match what really matters.

Next comes your vision. So your group on the island has this long list of values on their flip chart (if they brought a flip chart with them) and you next pose the question, "When we are rescued in about five years, our library will have already . . . what?" What will you do? What will you want to have accomplished? What do you want to *not* happen? For example, I'm sure you don't want that sentence to be, "When we are rescued in about five years, our library will have just run out of money," or "Our library will have just seen the last, disgruntled staff member quit," or, worse yet, "Our library will have gone through five bosses—one each year!" Yikes. Again, you see how important strategy can be. Take your dreams and use them to create your vision.

Now you're ready for your mission statement. If you research some of the best mission statements out there, you'll see that they come in all shapes and sizes. Some are longer than your average sentence, while others are short and to the point. One rule of thumb is that whatever the length, the content of your mission statement should be clear enough that every one of your staff members can know it—by heart. If your staff members can't tie what they do day in and day out with your library's mission, all of your work and theirs is going to be like tinfoil in a microwave oven . . . firing off sparks in all directions, with the meal never really getting done.

Once you get these key concepts of mission, vision, and values in place, you'll be able to move ahead, select a model that suits your library, and get to work. More on that next week. For now, you've got your work cut out for you. As explained earlier, these three concepts are nothing to gloss over. They'll take lots of your and your community's time, and the end result will be worth every minute.

Above all else, remember that what you're aiming for is excellence, and attaining that will be its own reward. It's your library's future. Plan it.

Suggested Reading

Nelson, Sandra. *The New Planning for Results: A Streamlined Approach.* Chicago: American Library Association, 2001.

WORKSHEET

1. **Start by making** a list of areas of strategic planning about which you are confident and elements of the process you feel less qualified to lead. Next to the latter, make some notes on how you can improve your skills and understanding in these areas. As the boss, you're going to be directing this exercise, and so you're going to need to be on your game.

2. **List at least** 25 things that your library values. It won't be easy, and you'll start running out after about 15, but keep going. Then, with that list, start prioritizing them until you have the top 10 values from which you and your staff would never waver. Are those written anywhere now? Did they influence your current plan? How can you rectify that, if they didn't?

3. **Where would you** say your community wants to be in five years? Where do you think the library would want to be, operationally speaking? Do these two visions match? If not, how can they be balanced and, if so, in what ways? These intersections of vision between you and your constituency will form the backbone of your library's future success. Once you've written them out, start making some notes on how your library can play a vital role in making these visions come true.

4. **What is your** library's current mission statement? Write it down (if you don't know it by heart). Now, keep researching until you find your very favorite mission statement that other libraries are using. Write it down. What are the differences between them? Which do you like best and why? How could your library's statement be improved?

Planning

WEEK THREE | YOUR LIBRARY'S STYLE

If you ask someone who has worked in five different libraries how many different strategic planning models she's seen, the answer will probably be five, at least. And that's a good thing. It's the organizations that take the time to find the model that's right for *them* that are most often successful. As was said before, you don't have to tell a librarian how many books on strategic planning are out there, with each one introducing a new twist on the basic format. But knowing there's a lot to choose from is one thing, and having the tenacity and the fortitude to keep changing until you find the right one is quite another.

As deputy director at my current library, one of my primary responsibilities is to manage strategic planning. When I arrived in 2003, the current five-year plan was coming to an end. In the history of the library, that was only the fourth plan ever written. The first, which turned out to be a seven-year plan, had been written entirely by the director and had, according to him, spent the entire seven years in a drawer of his desk, totally ignored. The second, also a seven-year plan, had been coauthored by the director and the board but met a similarly ineffective fate. Finally, the library began involving staff in planning and was getting more done as a result.

This was to be the third "traditional," broadly designed strategic plan, so we began to create it by mimicking the traditional planning process. We were busy forming task forces and initiating SWOT procedures. It was, after all, what most business leaders still agreed was the best method. In the *Harvard Business Review,* author Henry Mintzberg explained that "when strategic planning arrived on the scene in the mid-1960s, corporate leaders embraced it as 'the one best way' . . . to devise and implement strategies. Planning systems were expected to produce the *best* strategies, as well as step-by-step instructions for carrying those strategies out."[8]

WHAT'S SO "BALANCED" about the BALANCED SCORECARD?

In planning library services, the balanced scorecard requires a strategy that includes *all* aspects or perspectives of your organization's operation. For example,

Objective: Help Your Community Remain Technologically Literate

PERSPECTIVES	TARGETS
Financial	Allow for adequate hardware, software purchases
Customer service	Survey to identify learning needs
Organizational readiness	Ensure all staff have basic PC skills
Staffing	Expand schedules to allow for class instruction
Resources/collection	Purchase training, instruction manuals for support

But then, just as we were getting started and I was noticing those telltale eyes starting to roll, a letter came from our state librarian. It seems there was a group of librarians in California that was experimenting with a new, different kind of strategic planning model called the "balanced scorecard," and they needed guinea pigs to test it. The balanced scorecard approach intrigued us because it was more nimble than the old-fashioned model, because it was easier to communicate to staff and community, and because of the sharp focus it would allow us to take on each individual year. Because we saw a lot of shortcomings with our traditional method and a lot of benefits to this new option, we signed up and we've been using scorecards ever since.

For us, it worked, but it may not for your library. Remember all those books on your shelves? Strategic approaches are distinct from one another, and organizations trying to create and follow one that's wrong for them will be doomed to failure. We're all about measurement of progress, so we like the balance our method provides. It's a balance between historic measurements and projections; it's a balance between all the various perspectives of our organization; and, perhaps most important, it allows a balance in our priorities. We also tend to embrace change a bit before some other libraries, so we liked the dexterity and flexibility of an annual plan. While our library is comfortable keeping focused on what we *really* need to do during that year alone, your library might be better suited to a broader view. Also very important, the balanced scorecard helps us get the work done by strategically planning, thinking, and managing our future. But that's just one method and one library's view. You'll need to find yours.

You've heard that, in a job interview, you should interview the organization as well, to make sure it's a good match? Planners need to find the right strategic model for their system as well to help ensure success. Why does the model you choose matter? Mintzberg suggests that "planners should make their greatest contribution *around* the strategy-making process, rather than *inside* it. Strategic thinking is about *synthesis.* It involves intuition and creativity."[9] When speaking of old-fashioned, traditional models, expert Jeff De Cagna is even harsher. "Strategic planning," he explains, "is a dead end . . . [What we need are] new conceptions of strategy and fresh perspectives."[10] De Cagna feels we can't move forward successfully with the old models for "three basic reasons. Strategy and planning are not the same thing. Strategic planning is too inflexible and strategic planning is about the document, not about people."[11]

He is referring to the outdated models, remember, not to the process itself. So what's a boss to do with a library full of options, from binders to scorecards and everything in between? We took De Cagna's advice and found a new and fresh idea that worked for our particular library. So should you. Just as you would face any change, you should gather your advisors for a strategy session and start your search for the perfect plan.

You can begin your research with best practices or the traditional, most widely used models. The American Library Association (ALA) can help by providing step-by-step instructions to lead even a first-time planner through the process and toward a new future for their library. But remember, effective planning projects, whether traditional or specialized, *will* result in change. Part of your success as a boss is to ensure that both you and your staff are ready for that. As *Planning for Results* author Ethel Himmel explains, "The *Planning for Results* process isn't like a round-trip vacation but more like building and moving into a new house. At the end of the planning cycle, you're not back home. You've moved into entirely new surroundings that present new opportunities and challenges."[12]

No matter the model for planning that you select, the main elements of your project will remain the same. According to Sandra Nelson, author of *The New Planning for Results,* you will *prepare* (select the process that's right for your library and identify the people to be involved), *imagine* (hear what your community needs), *design* (establish your priorities and design goals to achieve them), *build* (identify actions and how to support them), *communicate* (write and share your plan), and *implement* (measure, adjust, and repeat).[13]

When you say it that way, it really does sound like fun. Next week, we'll talk about the end result you will be seeking—outcomes.

Suggested Reading

Hannabarger, Chuck, Rick Buchman, and Peter Economy. *Balanced Scorecard Strategy for Dummies.* Indianapolis, IN: Wiley, 2007.

Niven, Paul R. *Balanced Scorecard Step-by-Step for Government and Nonprofit Agencies.* Hoboken, NJ: John Wiley and Sons, 2003.

WORKSHEET

1. **Do some research** and list at least three different styles or models of strategic planning below. What differentiates them? What are the benefits and challenges of each?

2. **Find some articles** on recent, successful library strategic plans. What types of planning models were used? What does the literature say was particularly successful about each method?

3. **Get a hold** of a copy of *The New Planning for Results* and take a look at the steps involved in gathering community, board, and library staff input. Has your library ever done that? How might you do it again—or for the first time?

4. **Where is your** library's current strategic plan or, at the very least, the most recent one? Get a copy of it and, even if the period it covers is past, do a review listing the identified goals, what was accomplished, and what remains to be done. Just so you have a frame of reference going forward, give the plan a "grade," based on achievement.

5. **Sketch out a** draft schedule for creating your library's next plan. Start by assembling, at least on paper, your planning team. After working out this exercise, call a meeting of those people and involve them in helping kick-start a new planning process.

Planning

WEEK FOUR | RESULTS

They're called outcomes, outputs, work forms, action steps, activities, performance objectives, targets, and initiatives but they all mean the same thing—*results*.

You might be wondering why you need to spend an entire chapter of your development workbook thinking about planning. You are the boss, after all. What's all of this got to do with you? Well, hopefully you *were* thinking that at the beginning of this month, but by now you've figured out the connection. It's all about results. Think of all the good or even great bosses you've known. How did you know they were great? It was probably because of what their libraries were able to accomplish, right? It was about their results.

Everyone wants your library to be successful. Whether you are a brand-new boss or you've been in this position for a while, you want to be successful. Every member of your staff wants to feel as though they're making a significant contribution to the library and helping to accomplish something. Your board or your supervisor or whoever put you in this job wants to have made the right decision. Success is measured in terms of results, and results take planning.

So how will you tell when you've been successful?

In outlining the steps of planning so far, you've been asked to focus on the basics (mission, vision, and values) and the options of different planning models available to you. But here's the most important part—the part that many bosses leave out but that truly means the difference between success and I-don't-even-know-if-this-is-working—and that's the measurements.

One of the reasons the element of *measurements* is such anathema to most librarians is because much of what we do cannot be empirically illustrated. If a customer spends the day at your library working on her resume, then finds a job and comes back to thank you for being there to help her, how can you measure that? Or if a mother comes in to say that her child, who was thought to be developmentally challenged, just tested into kindergarten and she feels it's because of the wonderful story hours you've had, how can you measure that?

Don't be dissuaded. You *can* find ways to quantify that success. And, in reality, you must.

Once you find the planning model that is going to work for your library, just be sure you don't skip the chapter on results! One of the reasons my library loves using the balanced scorecard is because it "is particularly useful in communicating to the library's stakeholders the extent to which we've achieved [success], the trend in performance over time, and our performance relative to comparable libraries and relative to our predetermined benchmarks."[14] Why is the scorecard so easy to communicate? While some planning tools use narrative progress reports or traditional charts and graphs at annual intervals to record progress, the balanced scorecard suggests we share an ongoing "dashboard" or visual report that makes achievements easy to read and follow. Because it can be made so "readable," we hope that stakeholders can follow our progress from month to month. If you've never seen a dashboard used as a measurement tool, take a look online or check out some of the sources listed in this chapter. This planning model also utilizes a one-page representation of the library's objectives and actions, which is called a "strategy map," to help keep everyone from the board to the community involved in the progress.

It isn't enough for the boss to know where the library's going; there are a lot of other players who need to be kept apprised. It's your job to get your plan, whatever shape it takes, from the drawing board to the community.

Even in traditional planning, the emphasis on measurements and reporting of outcomes is critical. Draw a picture. Use all tools at your disposal. Be quantitative (tell how much or how often), as well as qualitative (tell why or how) in sharing your library's story. But "no matter which types of data you decide best meet your needs, be selective . . . too much data is worse than too little. The key to all of this is to be as honest as you can with the statistics you select and present."[15]

One important thing to remember, however, when planning your measurements is not to think you have to save the entire world (or library) in one day. As a matter of fact, take a lesson from Sam Davidson and Stephen Moseley, authors of *New Day Revolution: How to Save the World in 24 Hours*. Their approach to personal planning could be applicable in our professional world as well. "We all know that our best-laid plans of January 1 all too often become our easiest failures less than a week later," they explain. "What if, instead of saying 'I'm going to lose weight this year,' we said, 'Today, I will eat a salad for lunch.' What if, instead of saying 'I'm going to get organized this year,' we said, 'Today, I will clean out that drawer in the kitchen . . .'"[17] Imagine, then, if you were to say, this year, we're going to face this one challenge and, at the end of the year, you'll see our progress.

Eyes will no longer roll in your library in years to come when you talk about the *next* planning process you're starting, once they know that you know what you're doing and, above all else, you *will* make sure their work is all about the results.

TEN TIPS for SCORECARD/ PLANNING SUCCESS

(These suggestions will actually help *any* model of planning really succeed.)

1. Establish (and remember) where your (library) is headed.
2. Understand and stay current with what your customers want.
3. Define your scorecard and dashboard (strategic plan) rules and responsibilities.
4. Charter effective steering committees.
5. Establish and maintain accountability.
6. Link your scorecards and dashboards (measurement reports) to your strategies, goals, and objectives.
7. Communicate your personalized four-leg approach to everyone. (Consider all aspects of your operation.)
8. Use feedback and feed-forward loops.
9. Plan and execute your planning tool/balanced scorecards relentlessly.
10. Synergize your plan/scorecards for competitive advantage and new-market entrance.[16]

Suggested Reading

Davidson, Sam, and Stephen Moseley. *New Day Revolution: How to Save the World in 24 Hours.* Brentwood, TN: Xyzzy, 2007.

Hannabarger, Chuck, Rich Buchman, and Peter Economy. *Balanced Scorecard Strategy for Dummies.* Hoboken, NJ: Wiley, 2007.

WORKSHEET

1. **Again, like you** did last week, get out a copy of either the current or the most recent strategic plan your library has used. After reading it, list below the *measurable results* that came about because of it.

2. **Now ask yourself** this question. How many people in your library, your community, or on your board know about those results? How were they communicated? If they weren't communicated, how might they have been?

3. **If there weren't** too many measurable results, how might you improve on that? Are there statistics or evaluative tools out there that could have been used to demonstrate achievement? List each goal/objective below and what you could still use to document its success.

4. **It might be** time for you to start a new planning process or it might not. Regardless, make notes below to outline a *strategic communication plan* or model you can implement to ensure that everyone knows what your library is doing and why.

5. **Last week you** began assembling, on paper at least, a strategic planning team for your library. It's time to start working. (Even if you're not starting out on a fresh plan, complete these steps so your team can assess and share progress on your current plan.) Outline below the agenda for your team's first meeting. Try to make the first couple of gatherings more learning opportunities than workdays. Help everyone; first and foremost, get on the same page regarding what planning is, why you need it, how you're going to do it or are already doing it, and how you (and everyone else) will know when you succeed. Who will be responsible for which parts? Who will measure? Who will handle communications? Where will progress be reported? Be thorough. Be results oriented.

6. **Before you send** out the meeting invitation and agenda, select at least one good book chapter to copy (with permission) or article to cite to give your new team some basic info. This approach will let them know this is a *different* process than they're used to and that, as the boss, you are targeting nothing less than success! Read it carefully, and then ask your team to do the same.

Friends and Allies

WEEK ONE | THE COMMUNITY

Every single newborn baby in one nearby town gets a "Happy Birthday" gift bag, complete with board books, a stuffed animal, and, most important, a library card application, compliments of the local library. Seniors, restricted to their homes because of illness or infirmity, have bestsellers, as well as a bit of friendly conversation, delivered to their door. Volunteers comb the grounds at another library branch, weeding and mulching and having a great time. This already sounds like a great library, doesn't it? And we haven't even talked about what the *staff* contribute yet. So far, this is all about what your community can do for *you.*

One of the most frightening moments at work I've had was my very first day as *the boss.* Maybe you just had yours or perhaps it was years ago, but either way, I'll bet you can still remember that stressful, lonely feeling when you realized all eyes were turned toward you. You thought you were all alone at the top, right? Well, you were wrong. Among the *many* supporters you will discover throughout your career, perhaps no group will be as impressive as those who step out of your community to help *their* library.

To start with, let's consider your board of trustees. While most consider them a group to be feared and handled with kid gloves, it's the wise boss who recognizes early on that these people are the biggest givers your library will know. Volunteers all, they sacrifice their time, their skills, and often their patience to learn to work together as a group for the betterment of your library. In short, these people exist to help you succeed. Recognize them, nurture their skills and interests, and tolerate their shortcomings with grace. In the end, they are going to be a big part of your library's, and your, success. In her *Successful Library Trustee Handbook,* author Mary Moore says it best: "You are one of those truly blessed people known as volunteers. Surely, there is a special place somewhere in the universe for people who volunteer their time to ensure the public good. So . . . thank you!"[1] Your

SUCCESS with TRUSTEES

Library bosses sometimes delight in frightening new peers with horror stories about "Boards from Hell." It doesn't have to be that way. In order to share (because you both want this) success with *your* board members, make sure you *all* have

- a willingness to commit time and energy
- a desire to see the library assume an important role in the community
- a record of working well with others
- a willingness to make decisions
- the ability to participate in discussions without taking over
- a knowledge of the community
- the ability to advocate for and make presentations about the library
- a commitment to progress
- a willingness to consider new ideas
- a willingness to do the necessary work
- a willingness to help with fund-raising[2]

TOP 10 WAYS to BUILD COMMUNITY PARTNERSHIPS

1. *Join something!* Try the Chamber of Commerce, Speakers' Bureau, etc.
2. *Go to where the people are.* Take storytimes to stores or malls.
3. *Find customers who NEED you.* Grad students, teachers in grad school, etc.
4. *Tap your local colleges.* Get student interns or offer work for credit.
5. *Help those with whom you share customers.* Do you have a video store you could run a book discussion with? Could they provide coupons for prizes?
6. *Reach out to your government officials.* They need information, too. Find out how you can make their jobs easier.
7. *Give your seniors something to do.* Find projects with which they can really help.
8. *Tap youth organizations.* If you involve kids, you'll get their parents, too.
9. *Get involved in local politics.* At the very least, be at council meetings so they learn who you are.
10. *Barter.* Have the local florist deliver fresh flowers weekly, in exchange for a great "ad" on your circulation desk thanking them.[3]

board members need your help to grow and develop, just as your staff members do. So don't abandon them if their efforts become a bit myopic. Help them grow and develop right along with you so that together you can all succeed.

Next, as Joe Cocker used to say, you'll get by with a little help from those next on your list of community allies . . . your Friends! They're the ones who will sort through those never-ending piles of (sometimes) grungy donations—and emerge with a successful book sale for you. And they're the ones who will pick up a bag of books and drive over to a senior apartment building, where they'll share not just the titles but some friendship and a moment of their time. They'll be the face of the library for you out in the community and, when you need help putting together a special program or passing a levy, they'll be your financial friends as well.

Again, if you listen to those crabby bosses out there (they know who they are), they'll try to counsel you right into a frustrated cynicism about Friends. You're going to hear the same horror stories about some Friends groups that have gone bad. Like your board members, your Friends are also giving of themselves, including their time and energy and caring, to an institution they want to succeed in their community. Work with them, be tolerant of their quirks as they will be of yours, and, if you're really lucky, they'll return the favor. Is it always going to be easy? No but I don't imagine you expected *easy* when you took this job.

Your efforts will pay off. Even the ALA agrees that this invaluable group can make or break your library. "Friends groups," according to the ALA website, "can make the difference between a budget increase and a budget cut for their libraries. Not only that, but many libraries across the country owe their new additions or new buildings to an effective advocacy campaign waged by the Friends to ensure community support."[4] An aptly named group, to be sure.

What or who else is out there to help you be a better boss? So far, we've been talking about the community members who walk right into your library and volunteer, but don't forget, there's a whole world out there that will also get behind you, if you ask them first. Community partnerships or collaborations offer a wealth of support and allies for you, as well as expanded services and programs for your customers. For these types of partnerships, it's definitely a win-win situation. In *The Thriving Library,* author Marylaine Block quotes something Richard Rhodes said in 2005. "There is nothing community leaders like better," he claims, "than knowing that public entities are successfully working together. It gives them credibility and leads to other organizations offering to partner."[5]

You help them, they help you, and together you both get more support from others, maybe even in the form of grants. I think you see how this can go. Or, alternatively, you can stay in your office, approach the job like the Lone Ranger, and be overwhelmed and undersupported and watch one opportunity after another slip away. Don't let that be you. There's a big world out there that cares about your library just as much as you do. Let them in and make it succeed together. It's *their* library, after all. You just work here.

WORKSHEET

1. **List some special,** new, or creative services you'd love to offer at your library but you know there wouldn't be staff to support. Think about "Books for Babies," and so on. What could you do with "outside" help?

2. **Now match those** ideas to community groups, the Friends, other volunteers, or students who might be able to help you achieve these goals. Then, pick *just one* and outline the steps needed to put your plan into motion. (Include a realistic time line and deadlines so you really, really see this through.)

3. **Time for some** exercise. Taking this workbook with you, walk around the library and stop and ask at least ten employees if they can name all the members of your board of trustees. Back in your office, check your results. If they are dismal, list at least five ideas for strengthening the link between your board and your staff. Could you host a staff potluck, to help them all get better acquainted? What else might you try?

4. **You probably add** a new board member almost every year. Review your orientation packet for new board members. Is it complete? Is it exciting or dry? Does it clearly outline what you expect of your board? If not, update it and keep it current and vital. Consider putting your new trustees through the same orientation your new employees get. The more they know about how the library works, the better.

5. **Good board orientation** is vital, but so is ongoing exposure to all things library, so the members can continue to learn more and more about this world they may never have seen before from the inside. Look at your board agendas. If you don't already do this, could you add a five-minute staff presentation each month that would showcase a particularly unique or creative service the library offers? Make a list of the first five "shows" you could present to your board, and then reach the staff who would be involved and get them going on plans.

6. **If you haven't** already, put up a "Thanks to Our Friends" bulletin board in your staff room. Find someone willing to help you keep it current with pictures of Friends, news of upcoming activities, and past achievements. Once you're done, don't stop (ever) finding ways to ensure that your Friends feel valued and your staff know the community cares about them.

Friends and Allies

WEEK TWO | YOUR STAFF

As Will Manley tells us, "In the beginning was the word."[6] In his description of the creation of the first library staff from among the inhabitants of Sumeria around 3500 B.C., he explains that "the great thing about Sumeria was that for the first time since the creation of the world, young people no longer were limited to being either hunters or gatherers. Now, their futures were unlimited. They could be almost anything—irrigation engineers, mathematicians, businessmen, architects, even metalworkers. That left the small minority of young people who went to college and majored in the humanities and had no technical or practical abilities other than the fact that they were great with people! So these 'people persons' became the first reference librarians."[7]

If you are new to libraries and you don't know who Will Manley is, I would suggest you get some of his works to read. There is not, unfortunately, an entire chapter of this workbook dedicated to keeping a sense of humor in your work. However, in terms of career value, perhaps there should be. If there were, Will Manley would feature prominently under that heading. Look up some of his work. It will be worth your time.

At any rate, you have at your disposal, I hope you already know, one of the most amazing, diverse, creative, and inexhaustible resources at hand in support of your and your library's success—your staff. If you're smart, you'll learn that it's your job to point them in the right direction, remove all obstacles from their path, and then let them go. Is it that easy? Not always. But you can—and should—learn how to do that.

While this is a fun way to look at the life of the average library staffer, there are more serious aspects to be considered as well. You'll need to have the big picture. Your staff will depend upon you for their success as much as they depend upon themselves. Your people will always be your greatest resource. Treat them well.

The LIFE CYCLE of a LIBRARY STAFF MEMBER

Will Manley says library staff have "their own special series of passages":

- *Passage 1:* "I Want to Help Humanity"
  ("I believe in giving equal service to everyone. The lowest street person gets the same level of service as the mayor." Of course, if the stage-one librarian really implements that . . . sentiment . . . her future will be in the unemployment line.)
- *Passage 2:* "I Want to Help a Few Worthy People"
  ("Three months of being exposed to a diverse array of flashers, perverts, panhandlers, harassers, bawling children, and condescending professors will take its toll on even the perkiest new library school graduate.")
- *Passage 3:* "At Least I'm Getting Paid for This Madness"
  (The job, however, still has one redeeming factor—it is still a job.)
- *Passage 4:* A Reaffirmation of Faith in the Inherent Virtue of Reference Work
  (Yes, the satisfactions have been few, the frustrations have been many, and the compensation has been only slightly higher than what nonunion forklift operators make . . .)
- *Passage 5:* Reality Reasserts Itself
  ("The damage done . . . is more emotional than financial.")
- *Passage 6:* "Maybe I Ought to Transfer to Cataloging?"
  (This option proves unrealistic because "there are no openings. Once hired, catalogers never leave. Sometimes they die, but even then it takes a while to figure out that they're dead.")
- *Passage 7:* It's Time to Start Taking an Interest in the ALA
  (It's a "very big three-ring circus with a wonderful diversity of sideshows.")
- *Passage 8:* Don't Change Jobs, Change Titles
  (A new "information scientist" can be "wired with a new enthusiasm for her job.")
- *Passage 9:* Think Virtual
  (However, even with your "instant electronic access to a growing base of information in a wide diversity of sophisticated fields," be prepared for a continuation of "stone age requests.")
- *Passage 10:* "I'm a Lifer and Proud of It!"
  ("There is a certain serenity to be gained from accepting the inevitable.")[8]

Trust. One of the most important features of your relationship with your staff will become trust. Once you trust them to continually raise the bar and meet it, you'll be free to do your job and leave them to theirs. One of the most frequent mistakes library bosses make is to do their staff members' jobs right along with them. Usually, their desire to do this is honestly and earnestly founded on the reality that that work is what they already know what to do. The other "boss" stuff . . . they don't know so much. Learn to trust your staff's expertise in their own areas and you will be free to add to your own knowledge and capabilities as you get better at *your* job. The tasks for each are much different, and not understanding the distinctions between them can have dire consequences.

Picture a pyramid. Let's say that pyramid has three sections and each one represents different roles that staff play. At the base, the widest part, are the many members of your staff who have great task skills. They're the ones who meet the customers face-to-face and get the work done. They are your day-to-day ambassadors. Then, in the center of the pyramid, are those who have mastered those skills and, in addition, are capable of *managing* well. They can solve problems that come up, schedule others to accomplish the tasks, and so on. These are your department or branch heads. In the top third, then, are the bosses. Those people can do the job, as well as manage it, but they can also plan, envision, create, and lead change. They're the ones who will lead the others toward tomorrow, meeting challenges and exploiting opportunities along the way. They must let others do the "work" now because they're looking further down the road. They are setting the vision, making the community or legislative connections, getting the new funding, advocating with the stakeholders, developing and teaching the staff, and so on.

These are the bosses. That's you. If you don't recognize yourself in this picture, then you're probably slipping down too far in the pyramid. Think about it. Are you doing the boss's work or are you spending your time on the tasks that now belong to others? Do you trust those beneath you to do their jobs so you can do yours? Don't delude yourself. By stepping down to do the work of your staff, instead of your own, you're not only leaving them feeling unneeded, but you're leaving your work undone.

Trust your staff. Revel in their experience. Celebrate their skills. And stay out of their way.

Here's another way to look at it. In healthy organizations, where most people want to work, front-line staff members deal with the right now. Managers or supervisors deal with tomorrow. And true leaders or great bosses couldn't even tell you what is going on in the library today or even next week. They're busy getting a great future ready for us all.

Beyond those basic tenets, you have a lot of people who need to work well together, and they're depending on you to show them how.

What do you do with this great diversity of talent and enthusiasm? Your best bet is to build them into strong, effective teams. Teams provide you with a mechanism for bringing your best and brightest staff together and pointing them toward the achievements your library needs.

The authors of *Library 2.0* tell us that "it is imperative that all levels of staff within the library have the opportunity to contribute and evaluate ideas and services for your organization. These processes . . . can be handled by *vertical teams.* Vertical teams are team structures that include staff from all levels of an organization—from front-line staff to the directorial level, and everyone in between."[9]

You and your staff should decide what teams would work best. You could go the traditional route and have a management team, a circulation team, a training team, and so on. Or you could look for a chance to maintain a more creative and open-ended focus. Susan M. Heathfield offers what I think is the most creative division of personnel I've seen when she tells us about "The Five Teams Every Organization Needs."[10]

Leadership team—this could be your only "horizontal team," made up of your department heads and responsible for the library's strategic direction.

Motivation team—plans and carries out events and activities to build positive spirit among staff.

Safety and environment team—ensures safety in the library.

Employee wellness team—focuses on health, fitness, and so on.

Culture and communication team—defines culture and fosters communication.

Working with your staff on all levels, it's up to you to find the team structure that's the best fit. The results will come from the group. The leadership and commitment to put them to work must come from the boss.

Suggested Reading

Manley, Will. *The Truth about Reference Librarians.* Jefferson, NC: McFarland, 1996.

WORKSHEET

1. **Be very honest** and list at least three tasks you spend time on that are really the job of someone else in your library. Think about how you can let those tasks go. What do you need to do in order to trust someone else to do them?

2. **Now, just for** encouragement, list at least three tasks that *are* part of your job that you really haven't had time to do yet. With the time you gained after completing question 1, how can you begin to focus on them?

3. **List all the** internal operations' teams or groups that currently exist in your library and make notes after each about how effective they are or how you could "jazz them up" and reinvigorate them. Also, answer the following questions about each team. Do they meet only when it is useful? Do all your staff know what they do (do they share their minutes)? Is the team's makeup horizontal or vertical? How can you strengthen this team or, alternatively, disband it, and which should it be?

4. **What one new** team would you love to see at work, and whom might you tap to help you put it together? Set up a meeting with that person and do some brainstorming. What would the team's official charge be? How many people should be in the group? From what parts of the staff should they come? What could the first three goals of the group be? What kind of deadlines would you give them? Once you've established all of this—make it happen! And be sure you and they include evaluation in the process.

5. **Remember, all teams** aren't like the Supreme Court. They don't have to be in place for life. Often, day-to-day issues can be resolved effectively with ad hoc teams that meet a clear, short-term objective to solve a problem. Note one issue your library is facing right now that might benefit from an ad hoc think tank. What would their charge from you be? Whom might you name to the group? Sketch something out and share it with others to see if it would be worth a try.

6. **When was the** last time you helped your staff have fun and laugh? If you can't remember, it's been too long. Can you do something about that now? Today?

Friends and Allies

WEEK THREE | COLLEAGUES

When I applied for my deputy director's job, one of the first things I did was to search the library's website to learn as much about the place as I could. The first thing I found out caught me by surprise. The president of our library's board of trustees at that time went to library school with me—Yikes! I frantically searched my memory to try to recall how many classes had I taken with her. There had been two, at least. We carpooled once, I think. I sure hoped I'd never said anything too stupid in front of her. Turns out, I hadn't.

I share this story with library school students on the last day of their practicums with us. What I'm trying to tell them is that when it comes to formal references, most of them are ignored or, at least, minimized. The ones listed officially, that is. Area libraries, I often say, are like the Cleveland Indians or any other major league sports team. *Everybody* has played for *everyone* at one time or another. We all know each other. We're all colleagues. You never know who will be sitting in a position to affect your career and where, sometime in your past, you may have crossed paths with that person. So, given how important each and every opening is to my library, am I likely to call someone the applicant listed as a reference, who I know will give a glowing report, or will I scan their resume to find someone I know who might have worked with them? It's probably not hard to figure that one out.

The upshot, I admonish them to remember, is to make lots of friends, always be at your best in the professional arena, and leave as many people as you can with a great impression of you. Good enough, as a matter of fact, to hire! As you go through your career, from student to entry-level librarian to the boss, your colleagues can be your saviors, your lifelines, your coaches, your cheerleaders, or your doom. Everyone knows everyone in libraries, from the ones in their neighborhoods to even those around the country. If, as my friend used to say to her teenage sons, you use this knowledge for good instead of evil, you'll go far!

So how do you go about meeting everyone? Well, since they're probably not lining up outside your office door on most days just to catch a glimpse of you, the answer is simple. You get out.

Professional organizations are your best bet for starters, and, lucky for all of us, they offer a never-ending opportunity to meet our colleagues, serve our common purpose, improve our libraries, and, along the way, have a great time making really good friends. Depending on the amount of time and money you have, you can start local or go national by getting involved either in your state or regional library organizations or in the ALA or one of its divisions. "Librarians were one of the first occupational groups in the United States to organize as a professional association. The American Library Association, established in 1876, provided an ongoing mechanism for discussing, planning and developing cooperative initiatives."[11]

Everyone needs a peer group on which to lean. Even trustees, as author Mary Moore explains, need a place to go to regroup and reenergize. "While working as a consultant for the Washington State Library," she explains, "I instituted a state trustee conference that would occur every two years. At one such conference, a woman came up to thank me, saying 'I now know that I am not alone. I can't tell you how good this feels!' Let me assure you that you are not alone either. If you (and your fellow board members) need assistance, advice, or just a shoulder to cry on, there are people and resources to help you."[12]

And just as you need your supporters, your staff members need their network as well. Mentors. Fill your library with mentors. Be a mentor, hire mentors, encourage mentees and give them the time and opportunity they need to establish strong connections within your staff. Think of your staff as a golf ball, an interconnected tangle of connections on the inside that, on the outside, make a smooth and efficient product. The decision to provide support for your staff, to perpetuate it and to support it, can activate what Schreiber and Shannon call "a motivation cycle [that creates] relationship power and lights the fire within others."[14] They outline a six-step process to achieve this, which includes involvement, commitment, reinforcement, achievement, recognition, and, finally, motivation.

Being a naive new administrator, I remember my surprise when I learned that directors don't sit solitarily in their offices all day, alone at the top now and left to ponder all decisions by themselves. Quite the contrary: many of them are on the phone or their computers quite often, e-mailing and connecting with their colleagues across the state or nation, discussing issues they all share and getting and giving advice on best practices. Director or circulation clerk, we all need support. We need each other.

The best bosses know that and ask for help. Try it. As a side benefit, you'll have more fun too, and you'll get to know some of the greatest people in the world.

WHAT the PUBLIC LIBRARY ASSOCIATION IS ALL ABOUT

(The PLA is a chapter of the American Library Association. Other specialized subgroups in ALA provide similar benefits for many areas of librarianship.)

- "Provides visionary leadership ever open to new ideas
- Dedicated to lifelong learning
- Focused on and responsive to member needs
- Committed to a free and open exchange of information and active collaboration
- Respects diversity of opinion and community needs
- Committed to excellence and innovation"[13]

WORKSHEET

1. **Who has been** your greatest mentor? List all the benefits you've enjoyed by having this person in your corner. Make a "short list" of two or three new bosses you know of who might benefit from *your* offer to be *their* mentor. Then make the offer!

2. **Does your library** have a mentoring or "buddy" program? If not, should you? Do some research and find some good information on the benefit of these programs, and add a discussion about it to your next staff meeting agenda. Think it out first, so you can present a strong case. Who might be the right person in your library (if not you) to head up a mentoring program? What might the objectives be? Write out the three first steps that will get this program off the ground.

3. **What professional organizations** are available, both locally and nationally, to you and your staff? List them all and don't forget the "special" groups. To which do you and your staff already belong? Which others might you join? Why? How can you promote this? Can your library help with membership costs or time off to attend meetings or workshops? Create the outline (below) for a professional development plan and then call a meeting of an ad hoc staff group to get it off the ground.

4. **What skills have** you, personally, shared with your professional colleagues so far in your career? What else could you do? Teach, write, become a speaker? Make a professional to-do list below and then get started.

Friends and Allies

WEEK FOUR | CORPORATE CULTURE

It's been said that those who wake up in the morning to the realization that they're looking forward to going to work are the lucky ones. The truth is, it has nothing to do with luck. We all contribute to the "culture" of our workplace, and, especially if you are the boss, you can do a lot to *make* your place of business a pleasant place to be—or not. It's within your power and the power of your staff to shape the feeling of your library as a place of business. And it has everything to do with people and how they treat one another. Think about it. If you're doing your job well and establishing the right kind of work environment by rule and by example, going to work at your library will be a positive experience for all.

Whether you're going into a meeting with some board members, having lunch with the leaders of your staff association, or sitting in on the health committee's planning event, your approach and reaction to each should be the same. Honesty, professionalism, openness, and respect may not sound like political guideposts to many, but if you want to be a really good boss, they are what should drive all your interactions. Why? Because they work the best. That's how you promote and maintain a positive "culture." You walk the walk.

It's critical that you understand and are comfortable with the corporate culture you inherit when you become a boss at your library. Think about it. There might be things that need to be fixed or there might not. You better look around and be sure, before you fall into the same rut your predecessor might have left behind. What are the rules, spoken and unspoken, about how your library really works? In nations around the world, culture is established based on what people do, not on what they say. What do they eat, who goes to lunch with whom, how do they dress, who gets chosen for leadership, what do they do for fun, and, most important, how do they react to crisis or change? Should you support and continue the work of previous leaders in your library or are significant changes needed? If so, how can you go about correcting those errors—and fast? The culture or internal operations of an organization, Peter Bregman tells us, are "a complex system with a multitude of interrelated processes and mechanisms that keep it humming along. In most organizations, these elements develop unconsciously and organically," making changing—even improving—them challenging at best.[15] But certainly not impossible, and definitely worth the work.

One example of a culture in need of repair involved a woman who was told she couldn't miss a meeting scheduled for her wedding day; she'd just have to arrive a bit late at the church. Another involved a boss who asked frequently for feedback on his ideas but, since everyone knew he'd publicly lambaste anyone critical of his thinking, he, not surprisingly, never heard any. In still another department, there was a pervasive culture of dishonesty involving time cards that grew so serious it bordered on public theft. Don't be discouraged, though. There are plenty of positive, healthy cultures out there too.

We all know of at least one library where people stand in line to work! The one where, when an opening is posted, at least double the number of applications is received than any other branch would get. This is the library where the staff have been in place for many years and no one wants to leave. Now, what is it about that culture that is so appealing? I'm going to bet that it's largely the influence of the boss that makes it a welcoming and rewarding and fun place to work. There's no greater compliment to a leader than to be *the people's choice.* You can do a lot, politically and practically, to make that happen.

One milestone that Denise Reading suggests we aim for in reenergizing our library's traditions is to promote an innovative learning culture that features a "readiness for change. The investment you make in learning today may be the very investment that secures your future. It may be the catalyst for bringing your company [library] to the other side as a winner, not just a survivor."[17] Since we all know change is a constant on which we can depend, imagine the benefit of having your staff *ready* to succeed at whatever each new day brings. According to Reading, we should "create a learning culture now to solve today's problems and to anticipate and be ready for the creation of a new future."[18]

HOW to GAUGE (and IMPROVE) YOUR LIBRARY'S CORPORATE CULTURE

- *Test assumptions.* You think your staff know you mean it when you ask for input. Do they really trust you?
- *Ask questions.* Be nonjudgmental. "I see this differently. Can you help me understand this better?"
- *Listen to the stories . . . and create your own.*[16] What has happened in the past? What's happening now, that you want to share?

Picture first the type of organization you'd like your library to be, then make it so. You have a team of outstanding staff around you, you have skilled and experienced peers to lean on for support, and you have volunteers, from your board to your Friends, to support you along the way. The worst, absolute worst mistake a boss can make, it could be argued, is to dodge or ignore this challenge.

Anyone can look around and declare that everything is fine as it is. It takes a truly *great boss* to take on the challenge of making the organization better.

WORKSHEET

1. **What's the worst** story you've ever heard about working in your library? What does it tell you about your corporate culture? Have things improved? How, or if not, how might they?

2. **What's the best** story you've heard? How can you perpetuate the values and practices that support it?

3. **What type of** person thrives in your library? What are the qualities that person exhibits that are obviously a match for your cultural climate? What can you do to help more staff members thrive?

4. **Culture perpetuates through** stories. Share a story below that makes you proud because it demonstrates why working in your library is a rewarding thing. Shape the story here and then share it with your staff. Encourage them to send you another story to share, and find a way to keep this up (through a weekly newsletter column, perhaps).

Training

WEEK ONE | NEWCOMERS

There was something that happened to me on my very first day at a reference desk that shaped my attitude toward new employee orientation forever. It involved a loud, metallic clink. Or clank. Let me begin with a brief history lesson for some of you. Many years ago, there was something called a "pamphlet file" in libraries and, for local information especially, it was a very important resource. (This was way before full text, online.) It was my job, on that first day, to file some new materials in those files' drawers. My new library was a regional reference hub, with a larger than usual collection and staff, and was known or even renowned for its tough, professional "specialists." Two of them sent me to the metal cabinets behind their reference desk seats with my newly stamped materials.

At first, I was relieved to be able to find the right folder immediately, without having to ask for help, and I thought things were going rather well. But the drawer wouldn't close. Clank. I tried again, a bit more quietly (I hoped). Clank. After repeated tries, all of which I *knew* they had clearly heard, I gave up and, embarrassed, went back and asked my new colleagues for help. "Oh," they replied, "you have to hold the button in before it will close." Why hadn't they told me that in the first place? I felt doomed.

Today, I'm lucky enough to have the opportunity to help orient new staff. Remembering that day keeps me humble and helps me remember the most important thing about "newcomers" to my library. Helping them succeed is more important (although, arguably, less entertaining) than watching them fail. Everything you do, from the first day a staff member walks through your door to her retirement party, should be geared toward helping her not only succeed but reach, stretch her talents, grow, and be recognized. Your library will reap the benefits of all of her achievements, through her contributions and her modeling for other staff.

Where do you start? Just like with this workbook, you start with attitude. Whatever your orientation model is like, be certain it contains a healthy dose of "attitude expectation," so that your new staff member can understand the culture she is joining and her role in it. There are plenty of books out there on designing orientation programs. I won't repeat those steps here, but I will encourage you to spend the time to make sure you are using the best model available.

There aren't enough superlatives to underscore how important new employee orientation is. The flavor of the program, the content, the sincerity, the fun—all of it will set the tone for what could be the first day of a thirty-year career in your building. There's no denying that "the new employee's orientation, in particular the first day on the job, can influence how that person will feel about the library throughout his or her employment."[1]

Shortly after the file door–clanking incident, I made my second mistake on that first day in the reference department. Faced with about 1,000 reference titles that were all new to me, I resolved to go through them, one at a time, and commit their content and usefulness to memory. I figured I had to know the content and value of each resource in order to be successful with our customers. I started with 001.05 blah, blah, blah and headed for the 999s. No one told me that wasn't a great idea. No one suggested that you learn more about resources when you actually use them or that I should slow down a bit, take one question at a time, watch the modeled behavior of my experienced colleagues—or even that I should breathe. I was panicked. I had a lot to learn and my first day was almost over. Did I mention no one helped me? Don't make that same mistake.

Later, it was my turn to sit my new reference staff members down on their first days and start them off on the right foot. "Don't worry about how many resources you have to learn," I'd tell them. "Don't worry now about knowing what all those books on the reference shelves contain or how to manipulate all the online databases yet. If you want to be a *complete* success at this job on your *very first* day, just do one thing. Smile. Be friendly to our customers. Offer them the most enthusiastic, genuine, and outstanding customer service they've ever had and you will have succeeded in your job. All the rest will come later."

PICK STAFF with the RIGHT SKILLS

Before you even begin to consider reference talents, collection development background, or technical abilities, be sure the new staff you hire have "EQ," or emotional intelligence. (And make sure your own EQ skills are sharp, too!) EQ builds success, from day one. In orientation, focus your new staff on their

- *Self-awareness.* The ability to recognize your own emotions, know your strengths and weaknesses, and be sure about your self-worth and capabilities.
- *Self-regulation.* Knowing how to manage your disruptive impulses, maintain honesty and integrity, display personal responsibility, and be flexible, remaining open to ideas.
- *Motivation.* The need to strive to meet a standard of excellence, aligning personal goals with the group's goals, being ready to act on opportunities, and being persistent despite obstacles.
- *Empathy.* The ability to anticipate, recognize, and meet customers' needs, sensing what others need to develop and helping bolster them; to cultivate opportunities through diverse people; and to read and understand others.
- *Social skills.* Being effectively persuasive, sending clear messages, being an inspiration to others, being a good negotiator and nurturer, and creating group synergy.[2]

There are many and varied abilities that will make your staff unique and effective, be they old hands or new recruits. You hire with specific requirements in mind, most important of which is the right attitude toward helping people. If you recruit and attract the right people and then select the right people, you're on the road to success. To stay on that right path, make sure the very first day, the first week, and first year see them—and you—moving forward together.

WORKSHEET

29

1. **Take out a** copy of your current orientation materials for new employees and review them. On a scale of 1 to 10, with 10 being the best, rate them on the following criteria:

   Friendliness __________

   Fun __________

   Currency __________

   Professional applicability (i.e., are the resources noted still being used?) __________

   Thoroughness __________

   Inclusion/diversity (are lots of different staff members involved in orientation?) __________

   Focus clearly on library goals (do you spend too much time on dress code and not enough on customer service?) __________

   Corporate culture defined (will staff feel comfortable?) __________

   Communication lines established (what should they do with future questions?) __________

   Orientation evaluation/follow-up built in __________

2. **Now review those** scores and start making notes on anything below a 10. How can you improve your library's new employee orientation? Is it time to involve some fresh blood? What "special" features (such as breakfast with the boss) can you build in? Don't just hypothesize . . . make real notes and take some steps to get started!

____

____

____

____

____

3. **How does your** library recruit when you have an opening? What special steps do you take to *ensure* there will be diverse candidates represented in your applicant pool? If there aren't many, do some research to learn how others do it, or contact your local branch of a professional human resources organization and consider possible improvements.

____

____

____

____

____

____

____

Training

WEEK TWO | CAREER DEVELOPMENT

If it seems overwhelming to you that you literally hold a person's entire work career in your hands, then you're paying attention. That *should* get your attention. It should even shock you, at first, until you build your own confidence as a boss. But you should never take it for granted. I've been telling new bosses for years that even though we'll spend plenty of time talking about budgets and schedules and new roofs and Chamber of Commerce luncheons, *none of that part of their job will ever matter as much as how they treat the people they supervise.*

So is that it, then? Have you now assumed full responsibility for everyone's life and livelihood, happiness and morale, success and failure? Hardly. But you do have a very important role to play in setting your staff up for success. The part you leave up to them is whether or not they achieve it.

There are lots of things you *should* do, while helping to mold someone's career. You should continue to offer them ongoing opportunities to learn, for example. You should be constantly challenging their skills and gently, if possible, urging them on to new heights. You should be supporting them and encouraging them, but not all for just their benefit. You should be letting them do their job, and even make mistakes, instead of you doing it for them. Remember, the key to *your* job as the boss is to run the very best library possible for your customers. It's a simple formula, really. The better your staff, the better your library. Or as Richard Rubin once said a bit more bluntly, "The job of a good boss is to get work out of other people."

So you need to continually remind them that their success is their job; helping them along the way is yours.

Peter Drucker explains: "We live in an age of unprecedented opportunity: if you've got ambition and smarts, you can rise to the top of your chosen profession, regardless of where you started out. But with opportunity comes responsibility. Companies today aren't managing their employees' careers; knowledge workers

MANAGE YOURSELF with THESE QUESTIONS

- *What are my strengths?* Most people think they know what they are good at. They are usually wrong. The only way to discover your strengths is through feedback analysis.
- *How do I perform?* Amazingly few people know how they get things done. How one performs is unique. It is a matter of personality.
- *Am I a reader or a listener?* Few listeners can be made, or can make themselves, into competent readers—and vice versa. They will not perform or achieve.
- *How do I learn?* Indeed, there are probably half a dozen ways to learn . . . by writing, by taking copious notes, by doing, or even by hearing oneself talk. Know how you learn and perform but do not try to change yourself—you are unlikely to succeed.
- *What are my values?* To work in an organization whose value system is unacceptable or incompatible with one's own condemns a person both to frustration and to nonperformance.
- *Where do I belong?* Successful careers are not planned. They develop when people are prepared for opportunities because they know their strengths, their method of work, and their values.[3]

DURING OUR CAREERS, WE CAN GET STUCK BECAUSE

- We are not honest about the time and money a task takes
- We do not say "No, thank you" enough to those things that take us away from our most important work
- We are not allowing for slack, mistakes, and crises
- We let other people control us
- We don't ask for what we want explicitly and effectively
- We forget our mission
- We try to do it all; we don't ask for help
- We rescue others from the consequences of their actions, or we don't set consequences
- We are afraid to speak out, or we don't know how
- We take pride in being too busy and overwhelmed; we have lost the ability to determine when we are making ourselves sick from stress
- We have no criteria to use to make decisions
- We see competitors, instead of collaborators
- We confuse inputs with outcomes
- We think we have only two choices
- The plans are in our heads; there are no plans
- We do not have a way of measuring success and failure[5]

must, effectively, be their own chief executive officers. It's up to you to carve out your place, to know when to change course, and to keep yourself engaged and productive during a work life that may span some 50 years."[4]

One way of looking at a person's career development is as though it is the three-part pyramid described in a previous chapter. During the first part, the employee is "task" oriented. They may be very good at answering reference questions, processing invoices, or checking books in and out. This level of achievement takes skills, which require training and feedback. Some people choose to remain in task-focused positions, which is fine, as long as you continue to challenge them to reach for further goals, even if that only means faster service. Not everyone is cut out for management. Not everyone is interested in its unique rewards. Know your staff. But be aware of other staffers who *are* ready to move up, but may get left behind in this role, because their bosses aren't working hard enough to help them grow.

At the center level of the pyramid, your staff member can enter the management stage. People in these jobs leave the task functions totally or partially behind and move on to supervise others doing that job. Don't assume that someone good at a task will automatically be good at managing it. More training and support than ever is needed in this stage, to keep moving forward. Beware of the most common slipup here, in which the promoted staff member continues to do her old job, at which she's comfortable, rather than face the challenges of the new position, which seem overwhelming. She'll need your support at this point in her career. Help her grow and learn and, most important, help her let go and move on.

Finally, many careers can finish up at a position of leadership (the tip of our pyramid), which is beyond the day-to-day management job and into future planning, funding, and visioning. "Managers," a former mentor once told me, "solve today's problems. Leaders solve tomorrow's." Higher-level challenges and operations in this role require higher-level education, peer mediation, and training.

One trend you might be sensing at this point is that in most *healthy* or *functional* career examples there is a progressive development of duties, titles, and contributions that an individual will offer to the profession. As a good boss, it's your job to move that individual along at the right time and stay behind him *all* the time. Inertia is your (and his) enemy. Stagnation, in duties or locations, can drive the burnout bus right over the proverbial cliff. Bad bosses let their staff stagnate, while patting themselves on the back for having a loyal and long-standing staff. Remember too that not moving *up* is not the same as not growing. Staff comfortable in their task or their management or leadership position can and should be continually challenged to take on new responsibilities and reach for new challenges to support the organization.

Is your career moving along and/or moving ahead? How about your staff's? Thirty years is a long time to waste.

WORKSHEET

1. **Take out your** most recent staffing sheet and, next to each person's name, note how many years that employee has worked in libraries—both yours and others. (You might need to ask your HR person, if you have one, for help with this.) Now, look at those numbers! Pretty impressive, I bet. Are you confident that you, or their direct supervisors at least, really know what career goals these people have? Careers go by pretty quickly. It's time to find out. What are the first three things you need to do to get started?

2. **Thinking of your** "task-level" staffers, which of them do you think exhibit the skills and spirit necessary to move to the next (management) step? What training would help prepare them for that opportunity? Where can it be obtained? Sketch out a simple development plan that you can talk over with them, or their supervisors, as a next step.

3. **Now consider your** management team. Are any of them in need of training, support, guidance, or even just some good old-fashioned feedback? Do you know where they stand in their careers? List them below and make a point to have a talk with each of them to see where they are now in their careers, and where they might want to go. Then figure out how to help them. Whether they advance within your organization or move on, their success will be your success as a boss.

4. **How about you?** Since you've become the boss, have you let go of the old task or management duties you used to do? Have you truly turned toward your current job and begun developing the skills you need to succeed? Write the three biggest challenges you face below. Next, list all the strengths you bring to overcome each and to keep your career blossoming as well.

Training

WEEK THREE | KEEPING SHARP

I'm sure you've heard somewhere before that the difference between a rut and a grave is only about five feet. What they don't always tell you is how easy it is to slide into both. Before you became the boss, you had a big responsibility to keep yourself sharp, throughout your career and in any position, and guess what? You still do. But in addition to that, you now have that *same* responsibility for everyone on your staff.

Quick quiz. How many years ago did Elvis die? If you're like me, you're thinking about ten or twenty years ago or so, right? We're never right, we humans, when we try to conceptualize time. And we never realize how fast a career is going—until it's done. Trust me that, at your retirement party, you're going to be thinking, "Wait a minute. Didn't I just start here the other day?" Don't waste time. If I can venture two clichés in as many paragraphs, "Life is not a dress rehearsal!" For your sake, as well as for those who depend on you, make every day, every week, and every year of a career matter. While you're not assuming parental responsibility for your staff's success, you will play a role in their careers' success or failure. (Elvis died in 1977.)

First and foremost, you are a model. So model a growing, successful career. Before you go about espousing what *they* should be doing to keep sharp, think about what they're seeing you do. Do you spend every day, day after day, hunkered down behind your desk, shifting papers from one pile to another? Or do you attend conferences, host workshops, write articles, visit other libraries, and mentor new leaders? When was the last time *you* took a class? If the library school of your memory contained typewriters (mine did), then it's been too long!

One way to keep you and your staff sharp throughout your careers is to pursue continuous learning through certification programs. In many states, such as Ohio, there is an official certification designation process, with renewals required, for librarians. If your state doesn't have this procedure, do your research on how to start one and begin a conversation in your state agency about getting it going. With some of your peers at your side, you can approach your state librarian or your state professional organization with a proposal to initiate this type of development.

Outside of your state, the ALA also has great career development opportunities, for staff from directors to reference associates. You can find information on the Certified Public Library Administrator (CPLA) program on ALA's website. A relatively new program, at this writing there were 99 candidates enrolled throughout the United States and 9 graduates (including the author). The program is designed for librarians with many years on the job; the CPLA candidates average 10 years of management experience, supervise (on average) 24 employees, and are graduates of 47 different library schools. Candidates are given 5 years to complete the program, which requires completion of 7 courses in topics such as budget and finance, organization and personnel management, management of technology, planning and management of buildings, service to diverse populations, marketing, fund-raising and grantsmanship, politics and networking, and current issues.

Again, what's the point? The point is that career development takes a lot of forms. For different people, different levels of enticement and skill development will be needed. Don't ever forget, it's a long way from that first day on the job to retirement. Careers, like anything worthwhile, need to be nurtured, encouraged, and stimulated in order to grow. This new CPLA program looks to be doing all of that. One candidate explained, "The program appeals to me personally and in my position as the staff development coordinator for my library because I'm looking for a program that would provide training and certification for librarians interested in moving into administrative positions and wouldn't require obtaining a second master's degree."[6] Another echoed that support and added, "Running a public library nowadays is like being in business. Finances, budgets, legislation, technology, and staffing were not covered or have changed dramatically since library school but are now a necessary part of my current position. I'm learning as I go, but oftentimes feel over my head in these areas. The Certified Public Library Administrator Program would fill a void and help those dedicated to public libraries to feel confident with the business aspects."[7]

So now you have some options to keep your librarians and managers growing and flourishing, but whatever you do, don't forget the other large and critical component of your staff—those in all your support positions. In that category, we're all in luck because a similar skill-building certification program is being unveiled by the ALA for their benefit. It is significant that much of the work that takes place in a library comes from non-MLS staff members, yet often less attention was paid to their growth and development than to librarians. According to Camilla Alire, ALA president, this "innovative certification program demonstrates the value of all library support staff [LSS] to our national association and to our nation's libraries. LSS are critical to the success of our libraries in meeting the needs of our users."[9] Similar to the other programs, enrollees in the Library Support Staff Certification program will focus on developing skills in such areas as foundations of library service, technology, and communication and teamwork.

If you're *still* asking yourself what's the point, then I suggest you think back to how you got into your position as a "boss." Undoubtedly, you've had super-

WHAT GOOD IS CERTIFICATION?

Sure, it takes money, time, and effort, and what's the point? The Ohio Public Librarian Certification Program says the goals are

- to enhance, expand, and improve public library services
- to publicly recognize and encourage librarians, who, on a continuing basis, engage in professional development activities in the interest of providing better library services
- to assist public librarians in developing and improving their ability to provide leadership in a rapidly changing information and service environment
- to encourage and support the career development of librarians who want to prepare themselves as future library leaders
- to meet Ohio's public library service standards
- to underscore the dynamic nature of the profession in terms understandable to constituents, boards, government agencies, and legislative bodies
- to establish a coordinated approach to and enhance support for meeting the education and training needs of Ohio's public librarians
- to provide general standards to public library boards for use in personnel matters[8]

visors along the way who saw some skills or traits in you that just needed a little prompting, and they provided it. Some of that encouragement came in a formal way, perhaps through structured learning like that offered in these certification programs. Do they work for everyone? No. Ask any staff member who has recently returned from a training or development day what they learned and you'll get a variety of responses. Some come back with binders filled with ideas and unbounded enthusiasm. Others can't tell you specifics, but you can see they've returned feeling valued, because their library invested time and money in them and because their boss (you!) care. Aside from these formalized training programs, there are innumerable free, online options out there for every skill and interest. There's just no good excuse to not keep growing, no matter what title you hold.

Informally, you need to ensure that you and all the supervisors at your library are *there* for your developing staff. That means being a mentor. As expert Kim Bolan explains, good mentors act as "role models, career counselors, coaches and colleagues" who "guide and set examples, share time and knowledge, motivate, encourage and challenge and serve as both confidante and advocate" for both the mentee and for the profession.[10] All of these are worthy goals that create winners all around.

There's one simpler yet curiously effective practice you should consider setting up in your library that has proven to not only keep skills sharp but keep attitudes fresh and teamwork rich at the same time. And this system is free. Move your staff around. If you can imbed in your culture the concept of healthy change and sharing of skills and contributions, you'll have taken a giant step toward keeping staff fresh. There's little that can be as damaging as a group of people who've been at their current posts for double-digit years, experiencing the same customers, performing exactly the same jobs, exactly the same way.

When I've seen reorganization of personnel implemented because of emergency or crisis, I've always been pleasantly surprised by the positive results, and the staff involved in the moves have agreed with me, in most cases. So think about periodically changing assignments for your staff to encourage them to share skills, infuse new energy, and introduce new creativity throughout your organization. And do the same yourself if you can. What would happen, for example, if you worked out of another branch for a month or two? Surely you could find space for a temporary reassignment, and when you do, keep your eyes open to learn and grow with a whole new vantage point. Restricting staff (including yourself) to the same old desk or department or branch year after year after year, while perhaps the most comfortable arrangement for some, will most often result in a constricting dysfunction that's hard to erase and almost impossible to overcome.

Keeping sharp can involve organized and official steps or random yet effective opportunities grasped. For both you and your staff, each will be its own reward but remember, most important, the alternative to continual growth is that rut. You can do this. And so can your staff. The energy and enthusiasm that come from growth can result from small, concerted, and ongoing efforts. Look at what you're accomplishing in only one hour a week!

As we all know, ruts are much easier to get into than out of. Be a great boss. Don't assume that coming to work every day and the occasional pat on the back will keep your staff at its peak. To do that, it's going to take *hard work and effort,* from them and from you.

WORKSHEET

1. **Complete this sentence:** "I am a great model of ongoing career development for my staff because, in the past two years, I have . . ." (What have you done to grow and keep your skills sharp?)

2. **Do some research.** First, does your state offer professional certification for librarians? How about for others on your staff? If you don't find a state program, what's the next best thing you can find? Something at ALA or PLA? List the options here that you can share with your staff as development choices.

3. **Some of these** programs are relatively cheap and others are just the opposite. What kind of funding is available to help? Research some LSTA staff development grants and locate at least one that you're going to try for. Outline your plan and proposed time line for submitting that grant below.

4. **Take a good** look at the websites for the CPLA and LSSC programs. Is there anyone on your staff whom you might encourage to enroll? Make some notes below on who, how, why, and so on, and then get the ball rolling!

5. **Finally, what kind** of in-house staff development does your library offer? How about the library on the other side of the county? How important have you made development in the past? Make some notes below on how to approach this discussion at your next managers or department heads' meeting. How can you emphasize career development better?

Training

WEEK FOUR | THE FINISH LINE

There's nothing sadder than watching the last three years or so of someone's career wasted. You've seen this too, I'm sure. They've been in libraries for thirty years (or more), they know where every book is on the shelf, with no need to check the online catalog, they've tried every idea and can tell you which one to forget because it didn't work twenty years ago, and no, thanks anyway, they're not interested in learning anything new. They're happy to just sit tight, do what they've always done, punch the proverbial clock, enjoy the reduced fear of retribution that seniority brings, and wait for retirement. The brass ring for them is called FAS (final average salary), and they can see it on the horizon. In fact, it's all they can see. Or, at least, it's all they're looking at.

What a waste. As the boss, you know how important "a few years" can be. You need to keep your library and your staff moving forward. You need to get the most out of every single employee every single day. You need to bring new staff on board sometimes, but at the same time, you must be able to tap all of that expertise and experience that's holed up inside your long-term staffers who, like the tortoise and not the hare, are creeping toward the finish line.

Your staff needs you to resolve this too. Please don't look away and pretend you don't see the "elder" librarian not pulling her weight or not contributing at the same high level that's used to measure everyone else. Without senior staff to learn from, to be coached by, and to emulate, our industry would lose the opportunity to be better every year. Personally, I have always credited the many wonderful and skilled librarians, managers, and leaders with whom I've worked with much of my success in libraries. They've prodded me, encouraged me, and challenged me, shown me and inspired me, and sometimes even threatened me to constantly try new things and to find new ways to grow and serve our public. Today, my greatest professional joy comes from working with the next group of staffers and returning the favor.

You can and must demand a high level of contribution from your "senior" staffers. You can and must convince them there's a lot in this for them too. You "speak" for your newest staff members, as well as for your customers. And the good news is, you have lots of options!

Mentoring is just one option, but it's perhaps the most critical one. One of the greatest staff development achievements I've witnessed came at the end of a particularly successful internship program, during which I'd paired a longtime staffer with a new library student. They'd worked closely together on the creation of a local theater directory and the end result was a useful and attractive resource for our public. They'd worked side by side on the reference desk, where the student had clearly benefited from the amazing store of knowledge our librarian had to share. And they'd become friends. The student had convinced her elder that the next generation of librarians had lots to contribute, and the librarian had helped the student develop a strong and lasting respect for her elder colleagues, even those with paper shelflists! We began talking about mentoring last week in "Keeping Sharp." Keep it going. Your senior staffers are a gold mine of experience and insight, just waiting to be shared.

Teaching is another option that can open up whole new worlds for your seasoned staff, as well as for those fortunate enough to learn from them. It was recently suggested to me by a good friend that teaching makes a great *encore career* to follow on the heels of many years of public service experience. After all, isn't that a critical element of our new librarians' training? And who better to provide it than someone who has been out on the front lines living the public library experience for many years? "Good teaching," it has been said, "is as much about passion as it is about reason. It's about not only motivating students to learn, but teaching them how to learn, and doing so in a manner that is relevant, meaningful and memorable. It's about caring for your craft, having a passion for it, and conveying that passion to everyone, most important to your students."[11]

Imagine for a moment that we treated financial resources the same way we often treat human resources. That is, you have $1 million to spend on your library, but when you get down to the last $300,000 or so, you just ignore it, let it sit in your account, and never use it to do anything for you. In many organizations, that's what soon-to-be retirees courting the FAS seem to be. Can your library afford unused resources just sitting around? I doubt it. Tap their experience, encourage their input, and celebrate their ideas to improve your workplace. With all those years behind them, they're capable of initiating significant improvements.

Alan Robinson and Dean Schroeder, authors of a fascinating book called *Ideas Are Free,* say: "We believe that future generations will look back on the way we treat our people and be puzzled by the enormous human potential we waste, and how much that waste is costing us."[13]

A great boss won't waste one second of anyone's time. Not a brand-new employee, who is anxious to get started and soak it all in like a sponge, not a middle-of-the-road career person, MLS, or support staffer who is giving their all as both leader and follower, and certainly not a finish-line staffer. We can't kid ourselves that remuneration, that final average salary, will always be a key motivator for staff performance, but with the right leadership it certainly shouldn't be the only way we make our staff feel appreciated, valued, and always willing to give their best.

WHAT MAKES a SUCCESSFUL MENTEE?

Not everyone is anxious to have a mentor, nor will they benefit from one. Before setting a valued employee down a time-consuming "mentor path," be sure they'll be working with the right person.

A Successful Mentee

- is a go-getter
- is an open-minded listener
- is a good networker
- is a future leader
- is happy to be an apprentice
- is accepting of criticism
- has a great sense of humor
- challenges herself or himself
- is confident
- is resourceful and creative[12]

Suggested Reading

Robinson, Alan G., and Dean M. Schroeder. *Ideas Are Free: How the Idea Revolution Is Liberating People and Transforming Organizations.* San Francisco: Berrett-Koehler, 2004.

WORKSHEET

1. **Look around your** staff and identify those who might be cruising toward retirement or, even if they're not all that close, seem to have shifted to cruise control anyway. List them below and, beside each name, think of a project, mentorship, teaching opportunity, or other new assignment that might spark them to contribute more.

2. **Next, set up** some real meetings. Put them on the calendar, invite staff from the question above, and get some motivation going. Remember to be open to their reaction to your ideas and be willing to be flexible in *what* the new assignment is but *not whether or not there will be one.*

3. **While you're considering** individual staffers, think about some of your newer people who might benefit from being paired with a mentor. Pay close attention to Bolan's tips for finding a successful mentee and then start some of those conversations going to gauge interest. Write the names of potential mentees below and make some "appreciative" notes about what you'll tell them you see in them that deserves additional encouragement.

4. **What teaching opportunities** exist near your library for you (you'd be a great model for this) or for some of your other staff? Do you have regional or state workshops nearby? Could you host them? There's never a shortage of need for good, free teachers. List below whom you could contact with ideas and also which staff members you might tap for this project . . . including yourself.

5. **Finally, look for** training opportunities for all involved so that you can be sure you're setting your staff, both new and long-standing, up for success in these ventures. See if you can find, in person or online, some classes in "How to Mentor," "Tips for Teachers," or anything else that looks effective and appealing. List them below and get someone on your staff busy costing out options.

Funding

WEEK ONE | BASIC BUDGETING

A budget is a plan for getting and spending money to reach specific goals by a certain time."[1]

This just may be the one part of your "boss" job that you find the most frightening. And it doesn't matter how much or how little money you control. If you're running a department, you might be in charge of a small portion of your library's budget, or perhaps you're the branch manager or even the director and you're responsible for the whole thing. One marker of the difference between professionals and paraprofessionals in most libraries is that the former are charged with the responsibility for money. There's a reason for that. As the boss, you will be managing money, there's no way around that. As a *great* boss, you'll be managing it responsibly, knowledgeably, and openly. Whether you have frighteningly little training or a PhD in finance, you *can* learn to manage financial resources in a way that benefits your staff, your community, and your library *if* you stay focused on a few simple guidelines.

First and foremost, you will need to know (and admit) what you don't know. Always start there. Most of us didn't choose to go into library work because we're dominated by the left side of the brain, which is all scientific, mathematical, and logical. Most of us and our staff members are liberal arts majors, right? We live on the right side, which favors great literature and history debates. Most of us prefer a rousing philosophical discussion or a haiku performance to spreadsheets and advanced Excel formulas. In short, there's a lot we don't—or didn't—know about budgeting when we got started. It's all right to admit that. As a matter of fact, it's required. Just as with any other topic, there's an almost never-ending supply of books, articles, and courses out there to help us learn. Not to mention our more experienced peers and our industry's many organizations and chapters.

The greatest damage I've ever seen done in this arena was achieved by those who thought they had to pretend to know it all because they were the boss, so they stumbled along making one serious mistake after another like the Lone Ranger. Start by taking the most basic course or even a workshop in library funding. That beginning step should help you determine what further level of training and growth you'll need to do your job well. There are a lot of simplified versions and instructions out there. As with most complex issues, the best advice remains, keep it simple!

Keep this in mind too as you get started. Don't let history run your library. You're the boss. Don't be afraid to consider financial or budgetary changes. While you may be worried that you're messing with success, your ideas and new approach might be *just* what your staff and library need the most. Business concepts come and go. We've had *just-in-time* inventory, *one-minute* managers, and even concepts as routine as strategic planning over the years; all good ideas in their own time, until newer, more useful practices came along. See what's new out there and test your options. The budgeting model used by your predecessor for the past twenty years may *or may not* be the best path for your library to be on right now.

Lucky for library budgeters, we're starting from a good place. In a survey run by Public Agenda and published in a report called *Long Overdue,* the public's trust in our financial management and viability was confirmed. The report stated that "because most Americans believe libraries use tax resources wisely, libraries do not have to fight the 'cut the waste first' attitudes the public brings to so many issues of public funding."[2] We need to maintain that trust through careful budgeting. Then, when and if we must make the case for additional tax support, our reputation can speak for itself. "Even people who rarely or never use libraries," the report continues, "support raising taxes over other money-saving measures to help libraries."[3]

So let's go back to our first admission. It's time to answer some basic questions honestly. Did you know that there are four different types of budgets you could be using? Do you know what they are? Did you know that your library's strategic plan should be *directly* tied to your budget? What role does your county government play in your funding and budgeting requirements? How about your local school board? What about your state library organization or state librarian?

Chances are, you have a lot to learn. The good news is that your eagerness, your dedication, your experience, and your potential got you into this job and will serve you well as you add new skills and abilities. That's really why most of us accept promotions, isn't it? To continue learning and growing? So start with the best sources around you—your peers—and start benefiting from as much of their experience as possible. Then look around for courses that can bolster your knowledge and fill in the gaps in your expertise. While we're *still* not splitting the atom here, creating, communicating, implementing, and evaluating your library's budget is going to be one of the most important aspects of your job as the boss and will have a trickle-down effect on everything, *everything* else that you, your staff, and your library accomplish.

FOUR BASIC RULES about BUDGETS

1. A budget is a plan for spending money to reach specific goals by a certain time.
2. Any budget or plan is only as good as the time, effort, and information people put into it. Good budget practices should foster collaboration and exchange information among the budget team participants.
3. No budget or plan is perfect, since none of us can totally predict the future.
4. In order to reach our goals, all budgets and plans must be monitored and changed as time goes on.[4]

Suggested Reading

Dropkin, Murray, and Bill LaTouche. *The Budget-Building Book for Non-Profits: A Step-by-Step Guide for Managers and Boards.* San Francisco: Jossey-Bass, 1998.

WORKSHEET

33

1. **Make a list** below of what you *don't* know about budgeting and what you *do* know. This will help get you started on the path to learning and it will help remind you that you're going to need help here. Be honest and as thorough as you can be.

2. **Take out the** most recent financial report you can find for your library. Hopefully, it won't be too old! Spend some real, focused time reading through it—carefully—and make notes below on questions that pop up. Next to each question, note who or what you'll consult to find answers.

3. **Make a list** of peers, colleagues, and perhaps even teachers who could help you begin to sharpen your budgeting skills. Create a "financial learning plan" for yourself, and be gentle. You can't be expected to master all of this overnight. But detail how you will go about answering short-term—and long-term—questions and building your skills.

4. **It's time to** get started. Set up *at least one appointment* right now, before your one hour is up for the week. Who will you speak to first to start your financial skill-building plan? Even if you've done budgets before, this is not an area where you can be lax. If you have time today, start following up on as many other contacts you've listed as possible.

5. **It's also never** too early to get started building your library's *next* budget. What method will you use? Zero-based? Programming budget planning? Design an agenda for a management team meeting that can help answer this question and map out a plan for your financial future.

Funding

WEEK TWO | THE PROCESS

By now you know you don't have to be afraid of budgeting. With the strength and knowledge of you and your staff, it's going to be just one more tool you use to move your library or department forward. But whatever else you do, don't try to go it alone.

This is where you get your team behind you from the beginning, so that, from day one, they are both creators and, perhaps most important, they are supporters of the financial decisions you've made. Your library board probably has a finance team or committee that it uses to make decisions. Governments, from local city councils to Washington, do as well. If you've done budgets before on your own, now would be a good time to reconsider establishing an in-house finance team of your own. If this is your first budget, you're in luck. You get to start out on the right foot from the beginning. What will your finance team do to help you? Plenty. With representation from all departments and branches of your organization, your team will work with you and the library's staff to analyze needs, assign priorities, forecast possibilities, discuss, debate, and, finally, develop and monitor your library's budgets.

Look around you. If you are the director, then select some key members of your administration to join this special subcommittee. If you're a branch manager or department head, select some other staffers involved in your area to join you. Look for other talent as well. I worked in a library once that was fortunate enough to have an MBA on staff, in a "nonfinance" position. The organization was wise enough to include her and benefit from her expertise in most finance matters.

First of all, make sure you understand the ground rules of the process you're beginning. Are you required to submit information to another government agency? If so, by when and in what format? Does your board have polices governing resource allocation or per capita spending? What are they? If you have formal polices and procedures in place, it's your job, as the boss, to know and understand

DOs and DON'Ts of BUDGET TEAM MEETINGS

In Meetings, Your Team Should

- identify issues and problems
- generate ideas and suggestions
- hold brief discussions
- make decisions
- report progress

In Meetings, Your Team Should *Not*

- have long and involved discussions*
- gather detailed information*
- analyze problems in detail*
- do background work for problem solving*

* "Ideally most—if not all—fact-finding, analytic, and detailed work should be done by individuals or by small subgroups between meetings. In this way, only the results [and not the time-consuming process] are presented to the entire team during the team meeting. This strategy will free up time for the tasks for which the entire team needs to be present."[5]

BUDGET PROCESS STEPS

You've heard that even a walk around the world begins with the first step. Break the budgeting process down; it's worth your time.

1. Build your team.
2. Make sure you understand policies and procedures to be followed.
3. Choose the budget style that suits your library *today.*
4. Establish a calendar (that meets all deadlines).
5. Examine.
6. Plan.
7. Create.
8. Communicate.
9. Continually reevaluate.

them. You can change them later, if need be. But, for now, when you begin the budgeting process, they'll be your guideposts along the way and will help steer you toward success.

As your budgeting process moves forward, your next step is to decide what type of budget best suits your library's needs. To be honest, most nonprofit organizations, like libraries, use a simple, "incremental" budget system that simply increases the previous year's line-item amounts by a value equal to inflation. But don't feel compelled to use this system, even if it is the historical favorite. This is the place for you to learn about alternatives, such as zero-based budgeting or program budgeting, and this is the time in your process for your team to focus on alternatives. Do the research together, vet the pros and cons of all options, and pick the best process for your needs. Then get busy learning it inside and out.

The next step may be one of the most critical, as well as one of the most underrated, parts of the budgeting process. Establish a calendar! Why? Because, as we've said all along, involvement of staff members is critical in establishing buy-in. A calendar, designed by your team to clearly involve input from your staff, clearly illustrates to everyone that all parts of the budgeting process are important. Plus, it establishes clear deadlines. The more people you have involved in this procedure, the more important it is for everyone to know what part they play, when they play it, and when they have to be ready with their input.

Once you have an effective calendar in place, you can reuse it, year after year. It can remind you not to jump over sections, and it can remind your staff and board that, on a continual basis, their input will be a critical element in the library's financial success.

You are on your way, at this point, to creating, communicating, and implementing a successful budget that mirrors your library's strategic plan and will help you reach your goals. This is one of the single most important things you can do as a boss, whether you run your entire system or an individual department. Just like schedules, budgets are pieces of paper that we *can* master. But remember one more thing, once your budget is completed.

You have to go back to it, month after month, and reassess, reevaluate, and recommit to its goals. Remember, "a budget is an estimate of the costs for some activity over a given time frame. People tend to forget that a budget is a plan."[6] If you don't keep the numbers real, if you don't react to your environment and make realistic changes to the budget when necessary, then you've just committed the age-old librarian error of just filling another binder for the shelves.

WORKSHEET

1. **List the four** most common budget formats used by libraries and comment on how much you know about each. If you don't know enough, do some reading to get the basics. Now, which one is best suited to work in your library? Once you've made your selection, note it here and start doing some *serious* reading and studying to prepare your library to do it right.

2. **Identify members you'd** like to invite to join your finance team. Even if you have a group with which you've worked before, consider all the staff. Is there anyone you can add? Write all team member names below and note what they bring to the process. (If they're just there because of their title but they don't bring anything, think about excusing them for one year and including someone else.)

3. **Do you have** a budget cycle calendar? If so, describe it below and consider whether revisions could improve it. Should more time be given over to research and discussion? Do you scramble to meet outside deadlines? If you don't have a calendar yet, create one here.

4. **Next, list all** the things you've learned about budgets in just the past two weeks, as well as the areas in which you still plan to get stronger.

Funding

WEEK THREE | KEEPING BUDGETS REAL

The humorist Will Rogers once remarked, "The budget is a mythical beanbag. Congress votes mythical beans into it, and then tries to reach in and pull the real beans out."[7] In libraries, all our beans are real and there usually aren't enough of them to go around.

There are lots of ways you can take your library's budget to the next level of success. Although these ways may sound easy, especially if you're new to this, they aren't always. They involve those two key elements that can screw up even the most well-intentioned plans—people and history. How many times have you heard the words "We've always done it that way" used to explain everything from why you still fill out vacation request forms on paper, in triplicate, to why you keep invoices alphabetized in a shoe box (when they are also online)?

That's not real. Your reasons aren't real, the need is no longer real, and the result is a waste of resources, human and otherwise, that you now have to redirect into more effective practices. How can you do this with budgets? Simple. It's time to link your library strategic plan, or whatever they use in place of one, to the money. This practice will help you justify the elimination of unnecessary expenditures of time and money and will support the introduction of new, exciting ideas and opportunities. "Interest in the linkage of performance measures to budgets has been growing in the public sector for many years. The past dozen years, in particular, have introduced a number of elements that improve the environment for a merger of budgets and performance."[8]

You can start by energizing your team to take a *critical* look at the budget, not just a cursory review, with 3 percent added in for inflation, a strategy that many organizations use. Examine sacred cows and require proof that they're meeting established goals. And if they aren't yet tied to established goals, by all means make that change!

KEEP YOUR BUDGET CURRENT

- If you work with the director well before budget time to help create the budget, you'll have a better understanding of its structure and design.
- Do your homework about the real cost of items, and when you're dealing with vendors and contractors, drive a hard bargain to get the best price.
- Once you've gotten something included in the budget and realize it's no longer needed, *don't buy it anyway.* Always keep your budget real. That way, people will know to believe what you say.
- Ask again next year if something you want now is just not affordable.
- If an item is rejected from the budget but the situation is desperate, ask for it again![9]

If you library has three goals, all built around improving services to support your local schools, then adding the cost of a technology bus to travel outside your county doesn't represent a "real" need that supports your goals. Come budget time, even though there might well be a convincing voice at the table arguing for this expenditure, the answer should be "no" and everyone should understand why.

Another common limitation of budgets is that people are often reluctant to adapt them to their changing environment, thinking that once they're passed, they're etched in stone. Not true. As a matter of fact, that attitude is almost the direct opposite of what a healthy, honest budget should be. Budgets have to be amended, tweaked, and revised as time goes on because, in our real world, nothing stands still. All we need to do to underscore this point is ask staff to remember going through the recession of 2008–2009. At every juncture, it would seem, we had another cut coming down the road and we were working—again—on the budget.

The most important rule about budgets is also the simplest rule. Be honest. Always. Indictment potential aside, you have the integrity of your library in your hands, and it's yours to protect. In good times and in bad, you should always avoid the temptation to *pad* your requests or, worse, to waste them. "Study the mood of the people and the politicians and adjust your approach accordingly," author G. Edward Evans suggests. "During 'hold the line on spending' periods, let your request demonstrate how well you are cooperating. Do not try to paint too rosy a picture—play it straight, and do not try to 'put one over' on them. You may fool people once or twice because of all the other matters they have to consider, but eventually they will catch up to you. And when they do, you will lose any goodwill you developed over time and the service will probably suffer for a long time to come."[10] The "they" in this directive could be anyone from your city council to your board of trustees to your staff. This good advice applies across the spectrum and, if you follow it, you can never go wrong.

WORKSHEET

1. **List at least** five *sacred cows* here. These would be items that are *always* budgeted for and done, year after year, no matter the economic climate. Next to each, write what they accomplish in terms of your library's current strategic plan or spoken goals. If there isn't a connection, then go on to question 2.

2. **List the sacred** cows here whose accomplishment or contribution to your library you can no longer name. How can you get rid of them? To whom do you need to speak? What more effective ideas might replace them and what would they cost? Put down very specific notes here about how you can approach doing away with each of them.

3. **When was the** last time you wrote a grant? Remember how it felt to get it? Make a list here of at least three projects or items you'd purchase or undertake if you had grant money behind you. Then do some research on the first one. Who might fund it? Once you get started on this, keep going, project after project. (Get some help too. Place an ad on your circulation counters asking for volunteer grant writers from your community. Working with them as support can make these grants a lot more achievable.)

4. **So you can** keep the progress going from the above exercise, find a grant-writing workshop that fits into your schedule and budget. Maybe it will be online? Perhaps it will be a local college course. If you can't find one that works, then think of the bosses who work near you and call the one who has the strongest reputation for budgeting. Some informal mentoring can help your skills continue to grow.

Funding

WEEK FOUR | ADDING VALUE

There are lots of ways to assure your library's success and improve its future, and the good news is that many of them also involve money. *Value* is the name of the success game these days, and it will become even more important as our "traditional" funding sources continue to fade away. We have to add value to our customers' information needs by taking them beyond Google, add value to our local businesses by bringing shoppers into the neighborhood, and add value to our bottom line by creatively making . . . yep, money!

So how does a nonprofit, democratically free-for-all organization make money? Simple. All we need is a little help from our "Friends" and a whole lot of open minds.

Many of the *new* methods being employed by our more innovative libraries are considered a sacrilege by traditional, longtime staff. We're selling food and then letting people eat in the library? We're allowing baby showers and birthday parties in meeting rooms? We're allowing local artists to display and sell their works out of our "galleries"? This is where the open minds come in. The answer is, "yes!" and our libraries, staffs, and customers are benefiting from it all!

Explore all your options and keep your mind open to new opportunities all the time. Libraries aren't a commercial void anymore. Our libraries host hundreds of thousands of visitors a year, and if we can shake off the yoke of "never charge for anything," new business connections will stand up and listen. When our (healthy) vending company asked for permission to move their machines to a more prominent space in the library and argued that the move would increase their profits, we agreed *and* asked them to increase our profit-sharing percentage too. And it did! When our library gave the self-checkout vendor permission to sell ads on the receipts, we also negotiated another cut of the profit and a reduction in maintenance fees. And that "value" also helps us support our local businesses by providing direct, affordable marketing. Next, we plan to explore selling advertising in our monthly newsletters. These projects are "win-win" all the way around.

When no one could remember why social events are banned in library meeting rooms, our library decided to allow them in. Where else in our community, we asked, could one host a baby shower for fifty people—for $20 an hour and no cleanup? Our library visitor numbers skyrocketed and we saw new, "nontraditional" library users and supporters increase like never before. Also, I have to say, the money coming into the budget didn't hurt either! By meeting the needs of our customers through creative marketing, sales, and new partnerships, your Friends groups can greatly increase their coffers, which ultimately can help you fill those gaping holes in the budget. Let's face it: no matter how much you've learned over the past three weeks about *making* a budget, you're still going to be suffering if there's not much money coming in to support that budget.

And there's yet another route to adding value that you shouldn't pass up. You remember the urban legend that says there are millions of dollars of financial aid that go unused every year, just because kids don't take the time to apply for it? Well, maybe the same could be argued about grant support for library programming. Think about it. What do our programs do? We promote literacy, we contribute to higher school and testing scores, and we help bridge the technology divide, all things that funders and donors have historically sought to support.

For many libraries, it's not their feeling that grant writing would be fruitless that keeps them from doing it; it's quite simply due to a lack of skilled staff. Many libraries are trying to overcome that roadblock by advertising for *volunteer grant writers.* An ad from our library brought ten people out of their homes, most of whom had been laid off and wanted to keep their skills sharp, their name in local philanthropy circles, and, while they were at it, their neighborhood library prosperous. I don't know how much money is out there, but there's certainly more than libraries traditionally go for! One word of advice: use your grant writer volunteers primarily for the research and text-writing portion of the process, but keep yourself or your director involved as the point person, who makes the face-to-face contacts.

"Major donors are not interested in talking to fundraisers; they want to talk to the library's CEO. Money wants to talk to power. Professional fundraisers—development officers—are like Sherpa guides: they get the leaders to the top of the mountains by leading the way and carrying the bulk of the luggage. But library leaders must climb the mountain with them—fundraising cannot be delegated."[12]

REQUESTS THAT MOST FREQUENTLY GET a FUNDING "YES!"

Grants are most often provided to organizations that support these concepts:

- making a real difference in people's lives
- helping those not in a position to help themselves
- enriching the lives of many
- worthy projects not likely to receive other funding[11]

If this doesn't sound like the programming your library is doing, then you probably don't deserve the funding anyway. A trip back to your "community" drawing board is most likely in order.

There are a few key mistakes that you can avoid when you're budgeting. Especially when you're using "creative" budgeting with the additional fund-raising features just described, you have to be absolutely, positively sure that all dollars are being properly accounted for and spent. One author suggested that the number one mistake to watch for is "neglecting checks and balances. Many budgeting mistakes start because no one is monitoring accounts, double-checking records and questioning . . . Don't assume that *someone else* is keeping an eye out for mistakes. Ask questions and double-check figures often. After you have finished double-checking everything, a final triple-check would definitely be appropriate."[13]

If you don't do anything else, though, avoid the biggest mistake you can make as the boss, especially if you're a new boss. And that's accepting the status quo. Don't assume the budget method being used is automatically the best choice (there's probably a more modern model out there), don't assume everyone knows, helps with, and understands the budget (get a team together), and most important, don't accept that whatever monies have been coming in for years is all there is out there. Go. Look. Barter. Deal. Add value. Bring your budget—and your checkbook—to life and your library and staff will follow!

WORKSHEET

1. **List the ten** most recent fund-raisers your Friends group has held, the dates the events took place, and approximately how much money was raised. Then sit back and look at your list. Is it varied? Does it include new, fun ideas and possibilities? Could you even think of ten examples (you can only list "book sale" once)? Below the list, make some notes about how you can help your Friends broaden their fund-raising opportunities.

2. **Check your statistics.** How many groups used your meeting rooms in the past year and for what purposes? How many people in total visited your rooms? List the events you allow, followed by the events you disallow. Now, note the reasons why. Is it time to take this conversation back out of the closet and consider opening up your library to more varied community use?

3. **Describe a program** that you've always wanted to have. Maybe it's a computer or job-related training series? Maybe it's a local history or scrapbooking program? Include in your description an estimated budget, and describe the top three objectives or goals the program would have.

4. **What would three** outcomes of the program described in response to question 3 be? In other words, what would be its impact and who would be affected?

5. **Now, using the** answers to questions 3 and 4, you can write a grant proposal in no time. Do some research and find some organizations or nonprofits that support your type of program and actually write at least one proposal. Submit it. Good luck!

People

WEEK ONE | GROUND RULES

What you have to remember is that they call it "human" resources for a reason. As has been already stated, your job—as the boss—is all about the people on your staff. Not the DVDs. Not the programs. Not even the books. Your librarians and support staff have been charged with taking care of them. You're the boss and, as such, decisions that impact the day-to-day lives of your staff are in your hands.

"Human" resources refers to the incredible, immeasurable value contributed by the *people* on your staff. While dealing with, protecting, developing, and managing them can be an incredibly complex process, your one single goal should be simple.

Value them.

If you're lucky enough to have a competent HR person on your staff, you're halfway home. In many libraries, though, the director or manager is also the HR person. If this is you, I suggest you seek help. Join a professional HR organization (even if you have to do it online), go to a conference, or join a roundtable or HR interest group. Send out a homing pigeon with "I need to speak to a professional HR person" on a note wrapped around its leg. Or just call the nearest library that has an HR professional and find a way to barter the sharing of her skills.

Human resources work is not for the faint of heart. It often calls for tough decisions and challenging conversations, at least when it's done right. It's also not for amateurs, especially when it comes to points of law. Remember the reference in the beginning of this workbook . . . "I am not a lawyer. I am not a lawyer. I am not a lawyer"? Luckily for us all, the ALA and the PLA can be there to help when we don't happen to have a lawyer, or an experienced HR person, handy.

As the boss, you also have to keep on top of things, though. And "I didn't learn that in library school" is not an acceptable dodge. Take a class (the CPLA program offers a great one), read a blog, check out a book on HR law . . . do *something* to bring your skills and understanding up to speed and keep it there. But don't ever go that extra mile and consider yourself the legal expert, especially when you hold someone's future in your hands. Your smartest step would inarguably be—to make a friend. Look to a neighboring library or a local or state organization and make friends with people who know all the HR stuff you don't. Ask questions. Don't ever be ashamed to admit when you're puzzled. The true shame would come in the form of a damaged career or, worse, a lawsuit that might result if you try to go it on your own.

Where do you start? How about with your hiring process? You can't rewrite all your procedures in one sitting and you probably don't have to, but, as they come up, follow them with an eye toward evaluating the legality—and humanity—of your library's practices and policies. When you see something that raises a red flag in your mind, you'll probably be right to have an expert take another look.

Think about how your library hires new staff, from the wording of the ad you run (on what is it based, is it fair?) to the interview questions you use (do they really reflect the current job description, or have they grown into a "wish list" that doesn't even realistically match the salary anymore?) to the comparison of all your applicants' answers (how do you "score" or evaluate one candidate against another? Did you clarify the "right" answer before you started, so you'd have a clear measure to use?).

You shouldn't be concerned about legal issues such as these because you're trying to keep from being sued; you should care about them because you want to sleep at night. You should care about them because it's your job now to protect the interests, futures, and present situations of everyone who works honestly and diligently for you. These are some heady decisions you get to make now, as the boss. You get to decide, literally, whose family gets to eat and whose does not. It's not your *fault* that they all need work, any more than it is that they're not all going to find it. But it is your *decision,* and you need to trust that you're making fair decisions.

Raise the bar at your library. Ensure that your staff can see integrity in the hiring process by treating all applicants with the utmost respect, honesty, and legal fairness possible.

And speaking of *all* applicants, is there any diversity in that pile of names to be interviewed? If you don't *interview* diverse candidates, you'll never *hire* diverse candidates. So how can you make sure both you and your staff understand what that really means?

DON'T SETTLE!

When hiring, look for these key leadership traits in *all* your staff:

- strategic thinking
- execution (and proven follow-through)
- decision-making
- technical competence and expertise
- teamwork
- ability to inspire
- ability to (positively) influence others
- emotional intelligence
- creativity
- resilience
- capacity (and desire) to learn[1]

Other legal issues will come up. Have no fear that, as the boss, you'll be asked to decide everything from exactly what type of headdress fits in the dress code to what happens if someone needs six days to grieve a loss, instead of five. A lot of HR is black and white, law or not a law, and for that part, you need to admit what you don't know and call in the experts, before you get your library in trouble or cause a big hurt you can't fix.

Still, even more of HR work is intuitive, personal, and judgmental (in a good way). To prepare yourself to make those interpretive decisions, you need only have a heart and a conviction to respect your staff, above all else.

I can't help but share, at this point, the very best piece of hiring advice I've ever encountered. It is, if they're not *great,* don't hire them. If you find *good,* keep looking. Don't let an opening in your schedule and its resulting impact pressure you into settling. Jim Collins explains it this way: "Those who build great companies understand that the ultimate throttle on growth for any great company is not markets, or technology, or competition, or products. It is one thing above all others: the ability to get and keep enough of the right people . . . When in doubt, don't hire—keep looking!"[2]

Suggested Reading

Collins, Jim. *Good to Great: Why Some Companies Make the Leap . . . and Others Don't.* New York: HarperCollins, 2001.

WORKSHEET

1. **Gather copies of** all the interviews your library uses. Does each have questions that will demonstrate the qualities listed in the "Don't Settle!" insert? If not, write some new questions that do.

2. **List at least** ten different people, places, or groups that could offer you help or advice on human resources topics such as hiring or staff development. Be sure to include all contact information (numbers, web addresses, etc.), as you'll likely be referring to this page again.

3. **What is your** library's stand, policy, or general opinion of diversity in hiring? Read it over and make notes about how diversity *is* being supported and how it could be *better* supported.

   Already supported by:

   Could be better supported by:

4. **If you didn't** find anything in writing for question 3, then you are going to need to start the process to create a policy or procedure. Make some notes here on how you'll do that. Include asking other libraries for samples, doing online research, and looking for advice from some of your question 2 list in your plan.

People

WEEK TWO | POLICIES AND PRACTICES

Without boundaries, nothing can be measured. Remember, your job is to ensure that each and every one of your employees will succeed. In order to know that they did (or didn't), you have to have some yardstick against which to measure their actions. Human resource policies provide you with that yardstick.

I used to show new staff, on their first day, how my expectations of their work evolved directly from their job description and then, more specifically, from the performance standards created from that description and then, finally, from the measurements listed in their evaluation form, which matched their performance standards word for word. "You've been hired for reference work," I'd explain, "so you don't have to worry about receiving a bad evaluation because all of a sudden we found out you can't play the piano. Nowhere in any of these documents does it say you have to be able to play the piano."

There are few tools more valuable to a great boss than clarity, honesty, and consistency. A good HR policy book will provide you with a little of each.

Be careful how you write it, though. In many organizations, policies are written by management staff, not by outside consultants or experts, which can be a problem. While the homegrown intention might be in the right place, using the wrong words or leaving an issue cloudy is going to do your library more harm than good down the road, and using the *wrong* words can be even worse. If your library is smart, you'll find a way to blend in-house opinion with a proven, successful, professional HR approach. You can mimic some of the better examples of HR policies already in use and not completely reinvent the wheel to get started, but have an HR professional or labor attorney review your document before you adopt it officially.

To truly enrich your document and your library, add one more element to the creation of these guidelines: input from your staff. "More than anything, staff want and deserve respect . . . Workers also want a say in the way their jobs are crafted. After all, who knows better what is needed to improve a job than the people doing it?"[3] Management, staff, and specialists, working together, can help you build the framework for a healthy, functional organization.

Once your HR policies are completed, you should realize that they never will be, really. Change is inevitable—even in policy. Each year, you or your management team or your board (or all) should review policies and practices to ensure they don't need any updating or fine-tuning. But none of that is the hard part. What's most challenging is making sure your staff, each and every one of them, *knows* the policies, understands the policies, and, whether or not they agree with them, are clear on their own roles and responsibilities. That's what the policies are for. They *clarify* (remember . . . that's the first good friend of a great manager) what is expected of all staff.

Here's an example. One frequently touchy issue you'll have to deal with is punctuality and attendance. It's most difficult, I believe, to have the "you have to be here on time" conversation with a great employee who, otherwise, does her job very well. But for the sake of the team, you know you have to do it. You can't look the other way just because this person is your best researcher. "Here is where attendance expectations are spelled out in our policy," you should be able to explain, while actually showing her the text that was agreed upon by all staff and adopted by the board. Thus, this isn't just you picking on her for the last traffic jam. This is real, professional, organizational stuff.

Another example is dress code. Rarely will you encounter a more contentious issue. Creating an effective dress code policy with which everyone can agree is still like herding cats or nailing Jell-O to the wall, but it can be done. And when you're sitting across from someone with a "Screw This Job" T-shirt on, believe me, you're going to be thrilled to be able to pull out the HR binder behind you and point to "no vulgar expressions" in black and white. *Clarity.*

Be sure you and everyone who works for you know the rules. Always be certain to build time—and a quiet place to read—into each new employee's orientation program. Then give them your policy manual to read. It's their responsibility to know the rules, but yours to convey how important they are.

The next best friend of a great boss is *honesty.* That's when you can say, from day one with a new staff member, that they'll be dealt with according to established guidelines, expectations, documented performance evaluation, and predetermined consequences. If you don't have all of these things, get them. If you can't afford an HR person, then contract out to get your policies in place. With these policies, you can *consistently* be clear and truthful with your staff. The relationship you build will free them to perform at their highest level. And it will empower *you* to help them get there.

One more caveat must be shared here, though. If being a great boss were as easy as developing, sharing, and implementing a set of inanimate rules and expectations, then there would be no bad bosses, right? There's another powerful element involved here that only you can develop. Call it feelings or intuition or

WHEN MANAGING PEOPLE: AVOID THESE CHOICES

Management of others is about *them,* not *you.*

1. *Don't choose status over results.* Don't always be thinking of what's in it for *you,* or how you'll get your *next* job. A staff member's professional failure is not your own, if you've given that person every opportunity to succeed.
2. *Don't choose popularity over accountability.* Don't go to work to make friends—but don't make enemies needlessly either. The boss has to make tough choices; stay focused on your overall objectives. Be especially careful when you are considering internal applicants. Stay focused on the job requirements, not on a desire to make a popular decision.
3. *Don't choose certainty over clarity.* Don't, as they say, let perfect get in the way of good. Waiting for every single duck to line up in your row will more often than not end up with everyone missing opportunities for growth. Lead the way, and jump in first.
4. *Don't choose harmony over (productive) conflict.* Productive, respectful, professional debate inspires growth and success. Don't even try to please everyone all the time, but listen to those who disagree.
5. *Don't choose invulnerability over trust.* Expecting honesty means being honest as well. Admit when you're wrong and correct mistakes together with your staff.[4]

empathy or even just common sense, your staff will rely on you to impart decisions based on a combination of the library's policies and purpose, as well as your thoughtful, professional understanding. "There are no simple formulas or recipes for dealing with people. It is easy to see human resource management as the creation of rules, regulations, and procedures . . . but it can be deceiving if one thinks that once these rules have been created, people will manage themselves. Managing people always requires understanding them as individuals, and adapting to their particular wants and needs."[5]

WORKSHEET

1. **You need to** either start the process to create official forms, such as position descriptions, or performance standards and evaluations, or to evaluate what already exists. Consider what your library has in place, do some research on what other libraries use, and jot down your plan here. Do you need to pull together and involve a staff group in this? (Remember to include front-line staff, as well as managers.) Start with objectives. (Always a good practice.) List what you feel these documents should do, what their purpose is. Now go about sketching out what work is needed.

2. **Does your library** have an established disciplinary procedure as part of a human resources policy? If it does, review the procedure and make notes (below) on your impressions and areas of concern. If it doesn't, sketch out that work plan. Another work group is needed. Who will be on it? How can you research other library plans? What professionals might you seek out for advice? Outline the project here.

3. **Design a policy** review calendar that will allow you to incorporate a thorough review of all board and library policies each year. Draft it to match the schedule your management team meetings might follow. (Tip: Make sure to assign the initial review to small groups before the meeting, and ask them to submit recommendations for change or clarification. Don't ever try to wordsmith an entire policy in a large meeting.)

People

WEEK THREE | DISCIPLINE

I know, I know, you should never compare management to parenting. I've even said that myself several times. But human nature is human nature, and sometimes there's no ignoring the parallels. The fact is, everyone needs boundaries. Expectations must be clear. And most important (and we've all heard this a million times, right?), people need to know and believe that for every action, there is a consequence.

I believe it's in the area of discipline that great managers are separated from not-so-great ones. These are tough calls; this is an area where the true leadership of a boss comes through. Most of the time, the true measure of a boss is seen not so much in that she doesn't do it right (although sometimes it is) but in the fact that she doesn't *do* it at all. Ever. This is where it gets tough. You *must* be willing to discipline.

In short, great managers have to put their money where their mouth is. You have, as we reviewed last week, good policies in place to guide, reward, and punish behavior. It's your job to take those policies off the shelf and make them worth the paper they're on. Why? So what if you don't? What's the big deal if the librarian who is late at least half the time doesn't get suspended for three days without pay? Who's going to be the wiser? Everyone is. Who loses? Everyone does. Especially you, as the boss that the *rest* of your staff, you know, the ones who follow the rules, depend on. If you allow the motivation and morale of the rest of your staff to sputter and falter, it will eventually sink. And then that will be your fault, not the fault of the person who made the mistakes in the first place.

This week's focus isn't about *how* to discipline. It really isn't even about *when* to discipline, what words to use, or how much discipline is too much. (Although my next planned book, *Build a Great Team,* will answer a lot of the how questions.) Today, the goal is to come to understand that you *must* discipline, staying firmly along the lines of your established policies, because everyone's depending on you to do so.

As I have already related, the best boss I ever knew always said that when you see a problem, it's yours. When you hear about a problem, you can't pretend you didn't. You cannot look away, walk away, or not care. Not, at least, if you're really a great boss. I repeat this here because it bears repeating. And the toughest problems to tackle head-on, no contest, are those requiring discipline. There are a few guidelines to remember that will make this all a little clearer for you. They deal with the three keys to successful management of people. Not surprisingly, they're not much different than other management guidelines we've discussed. They are consistency, fairness, and respect.

While most organizations already have clear personnel guidelines, including, most likely, a detailed disciplinary chart, you may not. If you don't, then you have to start by creating one. Again, you don't have to reinvent the wheel here. Help is available from the ALA, PLA, and most likely, from the larger library in the next town. Get it in place. Make sure your staff know it, understand it, and see how it will benefit them. Then you're ready to apply it.

Consistency is key. That means, quite simply, if the person violating your rules is your best friend, you still have to discipline her. Or if the offender is your best librarian, you still do. Or if the person is your branch manager, yep, you still do. There's no escaping it. And, trust me, especially when it involves your friends on staff . . . everyone is watching! Nothing can be quite as destructive to your team as playing favorites or even giving the slightest impression that you may be doing so. Make the rules for everyone, including you, to follow. This framework will keep your library on track and will clarify what role everyone is to play in its operation. "Don't make excuses about why something cannot be done [when rules are broken]. Don't allow staffers to hand excuses to you, either."[6] Rather, substitute roles, expectations, and consequences for those excuses.

This pattern will keep you successfully in the next category—*fairness*. If this is the first offense and the consequence is a written warning, then that's what you give. Don't surprise staff by jumping to a three-day suspension without pay. Don't ever respond with a knee-jerk, emotional, or (worse) personal reaction that will circumvent your established system. Your policy and procedures exist to level the playing field and make life as fair as you can make it (although even a *great* boss can't pull that off with perfection).

When all else has failed and it's time to discipline, emotions can be running high. Try these tips from great CEOs:

How to See Clearly When Others Are Unfocused

1. *Focus on the real world.* The boss isn't always right. Use and trust reports, analysis, solid data, and hard research, even if they prove you wrong.
2. *Don't get emotional.* Don't shout, cry, or whine. No one wants to spend time with a boss who can't be level-headed in difficult times.
3. *Exhibit great calm.* Act like you know the world is *not* about to end. This is different than being unable to face the truth or acting like a know-it-all.
4. *Know that there is more time than there seems to be.* Many mistakes are made by bosses who think that decisions need to be made quickly every time.
5. *Continually build and support your team.* A very successful man once shared his secret to success: "I surround myself with people who know more than me."[7]

Finally, please consider, finally and always, the most important characteristic of all for applying discipline—*respect*. This is no time to let your emotions run away with you. Whether you are having a casual conversation with a staff member about a problem that will just end up as a handwritten note in her anecdotal file, or it is a more serious infraction that will affect that staffer's permanent record, treat everyone with consistent, genuine, and professional respect.

To set an example for the rest of your staff, to assure anyone who may be looking that yours is a unique place of employment where everyone is valued, you need to set and hold the bar high when it comes to discipline. Plus, you need to *ensure,* through training, coaching, and modeling, that your other managers and supervisors will do the same. And remember this valuable tip: "Coaching is not an event, it is a process. You can incorporate coaching into your current interactions. You do not have to always make more time to coach. Use the time you interact *now* as coaching opportunities. *Instead of just having a conversation, have a coaching session.*"[8]

Remember, above all else, the *purpose* of discipline. It is not getting rid of someone. It is not to punish or be punitive. It is simply to improve the staff member's performance and ensure that no more breaches of policy occur. You have a positive goal, not a negative one. You're there to help your staff, not hurt or banish them. If the result ends up to be the alternative, then that's due to your employee's response, not yours.

Your job is to implement the consequence that they knew was there all along and to let everyone else on staff see that it matters.

WORKSHEET

1. **Think back to** the last time you had to discipline an employee. Note the details below, such as how prepared you were, how well did it go, what was the hoped-for result, and what was the actual result. Finally, think about and note what you might have done differently or better.

2. **Okay, now think** about the last time you were disciplined by a superior. For many of us, it's (hopefully) been a long time ago, but I'll bet the house you still remember it! How was the interaction handled? What was wrong with your supervisor's approach or your response? Again, outline what happened below and then note how the incident could have been handled better.

3. **Does your library** have an official, written discipline policy? If so, get it out now and review it. If not, just imagine you have one in order to answer these questions. What is the most important element this policy should contain? What should it not do? How might it potentially help your staff? If it's done wrong, how might it cause damage?

4. **When was the** last time everyone who supervises anyone in your library received training or review on the right and wrong ways to discipline? Unless you say within the last year, it's been too long. Write two things below. First, what elements do you want the training to have? Second, how can you bring about the creation of this training, whom might you ask for help, and whom would you invite? Finally, get busy making this happen.

5. **Finally, for those** of you who answered in question 3 that you have no official discipline policy, it's time to start doing some research, and then some writing, to draft one (or recommend one, if you're not the director). I find it's more successful to tell your director, "I have a sample discipline policy for your consideration, along with the reasons it would be useful," than to say, "Why don't you create a discipline policy for us?" And if you are the director, you're going to need a draft to present to the board. Don't forget to ask your state library organization for help, or turn to the ALA, PLA, or peers in nearby libraries.

People

WEEK FOUR | THE ART OF NEGOTIATING (WITH ANYONE)

The word *union* scares most people, but it shouldn't. Think of it this way. If someone came up to you and said, "We'd like to begin using fair practices here," would that frighten you? Probably not. How about "We'd like to be sure all employees know what to expect from management"? Would that seem unreasonable? Or consider, "We'd like to ensure that our managers know just what they can expect of their staff." Nervous? Of course, these comments alone would not frighten you. But add the word *union* to these sentences, and then that's a whole different story.

Let's introduce the elephant in the room, when you're talking about unions. I'm going to just say it out loud.

Most *employees* think unions *will* let them do anything—right or wrong—and most *bosses* feel unions *won't* let them do anything—justified or unjustified. Interestingly, neither of these assumptions is right, *if* the leadership on both sides is professional and, above all else, keeps the ultimate goal of the library in mind. Sadly, this is often not the case, which is where library unions may have begun to get their bad name. Working together, though, great bosses and professional, unionized staff should be—and are—able to keep service to the public in their sights as their top priority. But somewhere along the way, things *can* (and often do) go wrong.

Here's how to prevent that, in *all* negotiations—formal, informal, and even accidental ones. Stay true to your shared goals. You'll find more than one reference to author Jim Collins in this workbook, and this might be one of the very best pieces of his advice I'll share. He calls it his "hedgehog concept." Simply put, it says that in order to be great (like a *great boss,* for example), three things must happen. First, you must identify your passion. Next, you need to be clear on what you do better than anyone else in the world. And finally, you need to perpetuate that which keeps you going, whether that's profit or funding or just balancing a publicly scrutinized budget effectively.

Life is negotiation. In all your work, stay focused on your passion, what you're best at, and what you need to keep going. To understand the importance of this concept, consider the following . . .

The Hedgehog Fable

"The fox is a cunning creature, able to devise a myriad of complex strategies for sneak attacks upon the hedgehog. Day in and day out, the fox circles around the hedgehog's den, waiting for the perfect moment to pounce. Fast, sleek, beautiful, fleet of foot, and crafty—the fox looks like the sure winner. The hedgehog, on the other hand, is a dowdier creature, looking like a genetic mix-up between a porcupine and a small armadillo. He waddles along, going about his simple day, searching for lunch and taking care of his home.

The fox waits in cunning silence at the juncture in the trail. The hedgehog, minding his own business, wanders right into the path of the fox. 'Aha, I've got you now!' thinks the fox. He leaps out, bounding across the ground, lightning fast. The little hedgehog, sensing danger, looks up and thinks, 'Here we go again. Will he ever learn?' Rolling into a perfect little ball, the hedgehog becomes a sphere of sharp spikes, pointing outward in all directions. The fox, bounding toward his prey, sees the hedgehog defense and calls off the attack. Retreating back to the forest, the fox begins to calculate a new line of attack. Each day, some version of this battle between the hedgehog and the fox takes place, and despite the greater cunning of the fox, the hedgehog always wins."[9]

In library negotiations, you don't find the reference staff on one side of the table and longshoremen on the other. You're all going to be from the same side—the library's side. When you get to the bottom line, you're all going to want the same thing. A well-supported, talented, and motivated staff that create the best library in the world. Your passion? A successful library that is well supported and well funded enough to continue to support services and staff compensation. So what is your library's goal or passion? Providing outstanding library service? At what are you better than anyone else? Creating a library that utilizes all the various talents of your staff. And what perpetuates you? A balanced budget that supports all elements of the organization fairly.

None of that sounds scary to me.

So whether your library is unionized or not, whether you're meeting with department heads or their lawyers or front-line staff representatives, you need to know and stay true to your *hedgehog* principles. You can start down this road by preparing well for all possible problems and by managing your HR situations correctly in the first place. You can do this successfully by playing the role of the negotiator who knows what she is doing.

The first rule is to *know your contract or HR policy.* Ambivalence and apathy are not your friends here. Neither is managing by knee-jerk reaction. Many, if not most, HR issues are emotional by nature, and when they occur you need to be the one with the level head who knows what to do first, second, and thereafter. In short, if you're going to make sure your staff (and your supervisors) play by the rules, you all have to know them. In most libraries, new employees are given time to review the library's policies and sign off on a document that ensures they understand them. Then time goes by. Do you still understand your disciplinary policy? How about the minute details of your time off or bereavement leave policy? You know what they say about bosses making the "big bucks"? Well, here's where you earn them. Read, reread, review, and train anyone and everyone in your organization to really know expected behavior and consequences.

The next HR rule is, *stick to your contract or policy.* Be consistent. I've said this before. Consistently. There's nothing more damaging to a staff than to see an infraction treated one way for one person and a different way for someone else. That approach implies favoritism at best and incompetence at worst. Neither of these are labels you'd like to have tied to your name. An issue, problems, disruptions in the workplace, and any other infractions need to be handled based on the incident, the contract/policy, and the facts, *not* the individuals involved.

You may actually find yourself taking part in the original negotiations someday, the ones that result in the critical contract or human resources policy. In that setting, the same rules of understanding, clarity, and consistency of goals will apply. For sure, you're going to find yourself involved in hundreds of day-to-day negotiations, each with the potential to have a huge impact on your organization, on your staff's performance, and ultimately on the relationships that exist within your staff. Be a leader in all of these interactions, whether you're at a polished table or standing beside a coffeepot.

How?

"What you have heard about leadership is only half the story. Leadership is not just about leaders; it is also about followers. Leadership is a reciprocal process. It occurs between people. It is not done by one person to another."[10]

Ultimately, what you need to ask yourself is who you work for. For your customer should remain your unwavering answer. Sure, you need to align the needs and desires of your staff with the goals and capabilities of your library, so that a mutually agreeable operation can result. But ultimately it's *not you against us,* and if it ever becomes that, then everyone is in trouble.

Bill Grace, in a presentation on ethical leadership, suggested that we all must contribute to creating workplaces made up of *gracious space,* where we can create conversations, relationships, and workplace environments that support transformational change. Most important, he suggested that great leaders (or bosses) should never be afraid to learn in public.[11]

Negotiations come in many different forms. Some are formal, held at a specifically designed table and including people of the legal sort. Others are casual, taking place in the back of a circulation workroom or outside the hallway of a staff lounge. All involve the potential to be destructive, impractical, and damaging *or* to be constructive, reasoned, and successful. Whether your negotiations will last a few minutes or a few months, be prepared, be focused, and you'll show all the naysayers that it *can* be done, whether you are working with a local in-house staff association or an international trade union.

Fear isn't for hedgehogs.

WORKSHEET

1. **Let's apply the** "hedgehog concept" to your library. With some serious thought, you can apply this process to your library and move from good to great! Also, you'll find that, with the hedgehog concept as your constant guide, you *can* stay focused during any and all kinds of negotiations. Create a Venn diagram to illustrate your library's shared, central purpose. For your first circle, define what your library is passionate about.

2. **Moving on to** your next circle (in identifying your hedgehog concept), at what can your library be the best in the world?

3. **And finally, because** we all have to materially perpetuate ourselves in order to achieve our first two circles, describe what drives your economic engine.

4. **Now apply the** hedgehog concept you've identified to how your library is currently run. Are you focused, as you should be, on those three circles and the points at which they overlap? Or are there things in the way that are keeping you a "good" library, but stopping you from becoming a "great" one? Answer this question first, and then start some notes on how you can make corrections, if they're needed.

5. **The last question** for this week is the hardest. It's time to apply the hedgehog concept to your professional career. Think about being the great boss you want to be. Describe *your* three circles and see where you are. (What are you passionate about? What are you best in the world at doing? What drives you?) Where can and should you be working harder, in order to keep your focus?

Leadership

WEEK ONE | LEADERS SHARE THEIR VISION

We can learn a lot about leadership from geese. Don't stop me even if you've heard this one. This is the perfect time to listen to it again, just as you are preparing to think seriously about what it means to demonstrate leadership. We follow leaders because they have, and share, a vision. Remember the old workshop question, "Why do you work?" After allowing a few moments for everyone to write down about ten reasons, the next question that follows is, "Why do you work hard?"

That's a lot tougher to answer. Usually, it's because you've found a place where your vision or passion fits the organization. Staff have to believe in the vision of the boss. Their leader sets the tone for all they do, every single day. If you're that person, whether you lead the entire library, a single branch, or even just a department, your leadership and vision are critical to your staff. You have to begin thinking about leadership by considering that.

You've seen (and heard) a pointed wedge of geese flying overhead before, I'm sure. Ever wonder how they do it?

Fact: As each goose flaps its wings, it creates "uplift" for the birds that follow. By flying in a "V" formation, the whole flock adds 71 percent greater range than if each bird flew alone.

Lesson: People who share a common direction and sense of community can get where they are going quicker and easier because they are traveling on the thrust of one another.

Fact: When a goose falls out of formation, it suddenly feels the drag and resistance of flying alone. It quickly moves back into formation to take advantage of the lifting power of the bird immediately in front of it.

Lesson: If we have as much sense as a goose, we stay in formation with those headed where we want to go. We are willing to accept their help and give our help to others.

Fact: When the lead goose tires, it rotates back into the formation and another goose flies to the point position.

Lesson: It pays to take turns doing the hard tasks and sharing leadership. As with geese, people are interdependent on each other's skills, capabilities, and unique arrangements of gifts, talents, and resources.

Fact: The geese flying in formation honk to encourage those up-front to keep up their speed.

Lesson: We need to make sure honking is encouraging. In groups where there is encouragement, the production is much greater. The power of encouragement (to stand by one's heart or core values and encourage the heart and core of others) is the quality of honking we seek.

Fact: When a goose gets sick, wounded, or shot down, two geese drop out of formation and follow it down to help and protect it. They stay with it until it dies or is able to fly again. Then they launch out with another formation or catch up with the flock.

Lesson: If we have as much sense as geese, we will stand by each other in difficult times, as well as when we are strong.[1]

Although it may not always be popular and is certainly rarely easy, *somebody* has to take the point, and that someone is the boss. "Leadership," someone once explained, "is taking people where they haven't been but need to go."[2] So where are you going (and are you taking your staff with you)?

Make sure of one thing. Your staff members need to know the overall, guiding purpose that you all share. Whether they like it or agree with it or not, it's got to be clear. Staying or jumping ship will be up to them. Remember, you don't get points for retention, you get points for success. So involving your staff in the journey is critical.

In my favorite library, we all knew that, without equivocation, we were seeking the holy grail of *excellent customer service*. That was it, in a nutshell or in the proverbial one-minute elevator ride. (Everyone should be able to summarize their mission or vision that succinctly.) *Every* decision, and I mean every move we made, could be measured against how it brought us closer to a model of excellent customer service. Whether your boss in this adventure is a great one or not, and whether you wholeheartedly agree with the destination, there's a lot to be said for knowing where you're going. And all along the road, *anyone* could jump in with an idea that was going to help us get there. Buy-in comes from ownership. Success comes from teamwork.

It's worth reminding you here of Kouzes and Posner's revelation (from the previous chapter) that "leadership is a reciprocal process. It occurs between people. It is not done *by* one person *to* another."[4] Ask your staff to help. Give them the *chance* to help your library achieve its goals and fulfill the vision. Their ideas and inspiration are the rest of the "V," remember?

Robinson and Schroeder suggest that in "high-performing idea systems:

1. Ideas are encouraged and welcomed.
2. Submitting ideas is simple.
3. Evaluation of ideas is quick and effective.
4. Feedback is timely, constructive, and informative.
5. Implementation is rapid and smooth.

LEADERSHIP PIONEERS

Aside from budgeting, marketing, scheduling, purchasing, and maybe even reference, great leaders need to be able to accomplish more "visionary" feats. How? By . . .

- *Challenging the process.* Be willing to seek out new opportunities, change the status quo, innovate, experiment, and explore. Most important, if you're going to do all this, be willing to treat mistakes as learning experiences.
- *Inspiring a shared vision.* We've been over all this, but it's worth saying again. Be expressive and attract followers by envisioning the future with a positive and hopeful outlook. Show the value of commitment to a common purpose.
- *Enabling others to act.* Inspire mutual trust and collaborative goals. Involve others in planning and give them permission to make decisions (and share ideas).
- *Modeling the way.* Be clear and keep everyone on course. Be consistent in how you expect others to act.
- *Encouraging the heart.* Recognize accomplishments and celebrate how they link to your common vision.[3]

6. Ideas are reviewed for additional potential.
7. People are recognized, and success is celebrated.
8. Idea system performance is measured, reviewed and improved."[5]

Leadership, by definition, means you are in front, forging the path your library takes. Your vision should be clear. It should be substantiated. It should be logical. But, more important, it should be exciting, passionate, and motivating. In a library class once where students were asked to visit a case-study library and ask front-line staff what the library's mission was, one response came back: "We're just trying to keep the doors open." Ouch. I don't know about you, but I wouldn't follow that leader any farther than the parking lot.

So here's the hard part. What skills do you need to do all this? You've learned a lot about practical skills in this workbook and, most likely, through a lot of other sessions you've attended or tools you've used. But leadership isn't "practical." It can't be taught. It *can* be honed, improved, and sharpened, but first it has to be in your heart.

Are you a leader? Most likely, even if you didn't know it, you are, or you wouldn't be in the position you're in. But there's a chance you're not, which suggests you might want to reconsider your employment, before you end up disappointing the many staff members who will look to you for direction and letting yourself down in the process.

Let's say you are or will become a great leader. Then get those leadership skills as sharp as they can be. Fly out in front. Know where you are going. Use the "uplift" of your staff to move easier and further. Make noise to support everyone and care about each member of your team. If they (or you) falter, and they will, make sure you stick with them until they're better.

That's what leadership is all about.

WORKSHEET

1. **In one paragraph,** explain your vision for your library.

2. **It's time to** walk around a bit again. Find at least five different members of your staff (and tell them you're working on a class assignment, so they don't freak out). Ask each person how they would describe your vision for the library. Jot their responses below.

3. **Now, back in** your office, compare your first and second answers. Have you communicated your vision clearly? Is it understood by those you lead? If your answer is "yes," list at least five things you've (obviously) done successfully, so you can congratulate yourself and make sure you continue doing them. If your answer is "no," list at least five things you can start doing *now* to get your vision heard and understood.

4. **Recognizing accomplishments of** everyone that leads your library toward its goals is critical. List the last five times you've done that recently, and if you can't come up with three, then plan three you can do *this week!*

You've got a lot of work to do . . . better get started!

Leadership

WEEK TWO | LEADERS MAKE DECISIONS

Good or bad. Right or wrong. Exciting or boring. Necessary or evil. Somebody needs to make the decision! *Any* decision! There's nothing more detrimental to an organization than a stall or bottleneck at the top, which stops everything and anything from getting done. Leadership means decision-making.

You've covered a lot of ground in the past year. You now know, if nothing else, that it's not easy to be a good boss. And it's even harder to be a great one. There are budgets that will need to be cut and people who will need to be disciplined, maybe even fired. And customers need to be assuaged, retirees need to be lauded, there are applicants to interview, and you need an aspirin.

What do all of these scenarios have in common?

You've got a lot of decisions to make!

So how do you handle the decisions facing you? There are a couple of different ways to go. In one scenario, you can surround yourself with competent, experienced people whom you involve in the decision-making process right up to the very end, but then you cut them out. At that point, you decide that *you and you alone* are going to be calling the shots. Be careful with this approach, for many different reasons. First, you'll leave a lot of good people behind and, once disenfranchised this way, their dedication to your organization will begin to erode. Also, this path sends a pretty clear message, but it's probably not really the one you want to be sending.

Imagine hearing *your* boss say, "Thanks for your help and insights. I'm glad you have so many years' experience and dedication and that you're creative and talented. Those are skills we value around here, but, in reality, I'm going to overlook all of that and just call my own shots. Don't worry, if things go wrong, you'll be back in the picture. But I probably won't be able to give you a lot of time to get it all fixed."

HOW to MAKE TOUGH DECISIONS

Social commentator Regina Brett suggests several options.

- "Write down the pros and cons of the choices and go with the best list.
- Business columnist Suzy Welch just came out with a book, *10-10-10*. It's a simple tool for making decisions. You explore how each choice could unfold over the next 10 minutes, over the next 10 months, and finally, over the next 10 years.
- Motivational author Stephen Covey offers this great tip: start with the end in sight. Envision the result you want first, then work backward . . .
- Ask yourself and others: What's the greatest good for the majority of people involved?
- Try to separate fact from fiction. Once you've done that, separate the relevant facts from the irrelevant ones. Nowhere on the table do you allow assumptions to thrive . . .
- Take a shower. Seriously. A few years ago a study published in *Science* magazine gave this advice: do your research, then take a break before making the decision. Complex decisions are best made by becoming informed, then letting the subconscious take over. That's why so many solutions come to us in the shower.[6]

This doesn't sound so good when you say it out loud, does it? You are saying even more, though, when you make decisions in a vacuum. Such as, "I'm going to tout this decision as totally mine. However, I expect you to adopt it, accept it, and develop it as though you were getting some recognition or acclaim for it, and as though you believed in it wholeheartedly, as I do." Still not sounding so good? That's not what you mean at all? This is one of those situations that can be more perception than reality. This may be *exactly* what your staff members are hearing.

Let's look at another option. What if you refuse to *ever* make a final decision? You might say, "Go ahead and set this plan in motion if you like, but I won't be publicly backing it or encouraging anyone else to go along. I'm not going to voice a commitment one way or another, since there might be some wrinkles left, and I'm certainly not going to be associated with any mistakes! Until you can convince me you are 100 percent certain it's absolutely perfect, count me out."

Whoever said "don't let perfect get in the way of good" was a genius. Otherwise, you're just going to build up that bottleneck that should be avoided at all cost.

What about a third option? How about if you build a great staff and then trust them to be a partner with you? You're a team, right? You will grow together, learn together, make mistakes and share successes together. If you let everyone in on the process, from the very beginning, all of your decisions and theirs will have a lot more weight behind them and a lot more support going forward.

Still, even with the right approach to decision-making, sometimes your team is just going to get stuck and it's going to be up to you to decide. That's the boss's job, and it takes the right person with the right approach to do it well.

Organizational speakers and writers will often refer to a sort of inverted pyramid model that illustrates the differences in jobs. Jim Collins has one as well, which breaks organizations down into five levels.[7] The boss—you—as you'll see in a minute, is at level 5.

level 1—the highly capable individual

level 2—the contributing team member

level 3—the competent manager

level 4—the effective leader

level 5—the executive

At level 1, you have those members of your staff who are good at the tasks that you need to have done and done well. This could be your best reference librarian, or the building department person who keeps your library spotless, or the circulation assistant who knows your online system from front to back. Your library couldn't survive without these people. Their skills are irreplaceable. Collins explains that these individuals demonstrate "talent, knowledge, skills and good work habits."[8]

At level 2, you find your valuable team members. Those are the people who *both* do their own jobs well and influence those around them to excel and grow and contribute even more. Most staff at this level don't necessarily have *titles* to indicate their position, but if you're trying to build consensus, you know they're the ones to go to.

Your organization's first group of *bosses,* often department heads or branch managers, are found at level 3. They know how to accomplish necessary tasks, motivate and lead teams, *and* "organize people and resources to meet objectives."[9] If you need your managers on the circulation or reference desk, they can do it. But they can also schedule, budget, and handle planning issues to ensure that others can do the work as well.

Higher-level bosses are at level 4. They have also mastered the tasks that make up your operation, they possess team-building skills, and they can manage people and resources. Beyond that, they "catalyze commitment to and vigorous pursuit of" your library's vision. They model good performance and develop continual improvement in others.

Level 5 is the ultimate boss. In most libraries this will be, or at least should be, the director. They, obviously, can do all of the above, but they understand those tasks now belong to their skilled staff. Their job is to not only pursue the organization's vision, but to create it.

When the time comes to conclude who will be involved in the decision-making and what kind of input you'll need, consider all of these factors, and then consider this one last thought.

You can't always be right. You can't always know when it's time to close the discussion and decide. There is, no matter how much study you make, no magic potion or crystal ball you can use to avoid mistakes. There's really only one final thing you're going to have to do. On those occasions, hold your breath and take your best shot. Make the decision. Your staff will come to depend on you, to trust you, and to admire the courage it takes to be the decision-maker they all need. Rest assured that making *any* decision, even a bad one, is better—always better—than making no decision at all. I'll repeat again that it pays to remember that *no mistake is final.*

DIFFERENT KINDS of DECISIONS

In any team, there are decisions and there are decisions. Some benefit from broad input. Some will improve with discussion and debate. Others just need to be made. As long as you are clear and honest about which is which—and why—your team will remain strong. Remember, ultimately, someone must decide. That's the job of the boss.

- *Telling.* "Okay, team, here's the problem. Here's the solution. Here's what I want you do to. Do it."
- *Selling.* "Here's the problem. Here's the solution. Here's why I came to it. Now do it."
- *Testing.* "Here's the problem. Here's *my* solution. What do *you* think?"
- *Consulting.* "Here's the problem. I have no solution. I have some ideas, but I'd like to hear from you."
- *Co-creating.* "Here's the problem. Let's make the decision together."[10]

WORKSHEET

1. **Write down the** very best decision you've made in the past year. Knowing how many different ways there are to make decisions and how many different people may or may not be involved, describe how you arrived at this one. Then consider what you might have done better.

2. **Do the same** as for question 1 above, but this time, write down the worst decision you've made in the past year. What were the consequences which you would have preferred to avoid? How did you arrive at the decision and how might you do it differently, if you could do it over?

3. **Once more, looking** back over the last year, write down one example of a time when you needed to make a decision but didn't. Why? How would you approach that opportunity now, if you could repeat it?

4. **List the most** significant decision you're facing right now. Describe it fully, including the consequences it could have on your organization, then note what type of decision it is (telling, selling, testing, consulting, or co-creating) and what level of decision-making it should include (considering levels 1–5). Finally, write down the next step you're going to take in each instance.

   A. **Decision 1:** ____________

   B. **Type:** ____________

   C. **Level:** ____________

   D. **Next step:** ____________

Leadership

WEEK THREE | LEADERS TAKE ACTION

One day, there were three birds sitting on a telephone wire, looking around the neighborhood. Two of them decided it was time to fly away. How many were left?

If you've heard that one, you know the answer is not one. It's three. There were *all three* left because the first two didn't ever *do* anything; they didn't take any *action,* they just made the decision.

Over the course of this year, as you've worked in a lot of areas of this development program, you've (hopefully) learned a lot of things. Things about preparation. Things about planning. Things about consensus and human behavior and even decision-making. What you need to keep in mind is that none of those things will be worth the paper they're written on unless somebody (you) actually does something!

So what's the best way to ensure that you and your staff will take action and get off the telephone wire? You have to keep them moving forward. There is no finish line in leadership. You are going to have to make decisions turn into action. You'll help teach, design, and coach all the way through project management. And in addition to being out in front of the curve, you'll also have to hang back sometimes and just be the cheering section.

After a long and (understandably) grueling switch-over from one integrated library system to another, an exhausted staff member hopefully asked her director, "Can that be it for a while? Can you quit with all these changes now so we can relax?" The bad news is, the answer is "no." The good news is, the answer is "no." What that director needed to do right then and there was use this excellent question as a springboard to a discussion on innovative cultures—and how they create greatness.

A regional library system, now defunct, once captured that concept perfectly in an advertisement for a workshop on ethical leadership. The presenter, Bill Grace, was going to share his concept of something called "gracious space." The ad suggested we all needed to "create conversations, relationships, and workplace environments that support transformational change."[11]

At the workshop Grace, then executive director of the Center for Ethical Leadership in Seattle, urged those of us in attendance to embrace this inspirational concept in order to create our own innovative cultures. The word *transformational* is the key. "Leaders," he said, "create environments."[12] He further explained why *transformational* change was a good thing and one that the director above should have used the staff member's question to embrace. Grace explained that while we usually *transact* business or *do things right,* a transformational culture would encourage us to *do the right thing.*

Our reality, though, is that many people fear change, especially the transformational kind. So how can leaders support innovation? You must be sure that neither you, nor your staff members, fear failure. With change, there is always uncertainty. Is this the right thing to do? Will this new system or practice or service meet changing needs? Should we take this chance, or would it be safer to just stick with the status quo, and see what happens? Great bosses have to be able to convince their staffs that the alternative to failure is far worse.

"To swear off making mistakes is very easy. All you have to do is swear off having ideas."[13] Who wants to do that? Action will sometimes result in failure, there's no arguing that. But, often, it won't. Whether it does or not, as your staff sees you time and again standing behind them, picking up the pieces, making the adjustments, and continuing to move forward, your culture of innovation will be strengthened.

For one thing, a culture that embraces change and innovation needs to have the right people in it. Yep, we're back on that bus again. But what if you're a new boss and, all around you, you feel and hear distrust, fear of change, and, worse yet, apathy? Wait! Don't fire the whole staff! Every single person on your staff has the *potential,* as my good friend used to say about her teenagers, to use their powers for good instead of evil. You can win their trust by articulating your vision, sharing the future you see, and demonstrating that, step by step, you know how to get them there. "If the plan is in your head, there is no plan."[14] Spell it out for them and then, if they still aren't on board, you're going to have to take broader action.

Back to the bus: you're driving, so start with yourself. Don't administer—innovate. Don't imitate—originate. Don't maintain—develop. Don't focus on the system—focus on the people. Don't rely on control—inspire trust. Don't keep your eye on the bottom line—keep your eye on the horizon.[16] With these steps you will not only be advocating innovation, you'll be modeling it.

Bringing your staff along can be a lot harder, no argument there. Keeping the future of your library in mind, consider offering them a chance to see the library from different perspectives than the predictable, historical, somewhat closed culture they're probably used to. The authors of *Library 2.0* suggest staffing ideas that, while commonplace in the private sector, might seem revolutionary in libraries. Still, nobody said it was easy to change a culture. Consider:

CREATE an INNOVATIVE CULTURE

It's up to you, the boss, to convince your staff that yours is an innovation culture. Stephen Abram offers several ways to accomplish this, including . . .

- *Have a vision—and dream big.* The power of vision is critical—always be future-focused.
- *Good, not perfect.* Break the perfectionist mind-set that characterizes so many in our field. Be willing to take chances, before everything on the drawing board is perfect.
- *Avoid delays between steps.* A well-outlined project management plan allows for testing and reflection, but it also highlights intermediate milestones along the way so progress can be sure and steady.
- *Prefer action over study.* If you and your staff get caught up studying a potential change to death—remember that death was not the original goal.
- *Use the 70/30 rule.* Consensus is needed to move a change forward, surely, but consensus does not mean everyone agrees. Try to get to a point where everyone likes about 70 percent of the plan—and can live with the other 30 percent.
- *Don't assume—test.* Yes, we know our customers, but we can't know what they might like *next.* And, yes, that didn't work when we tried it five years ago, but that doesn't mean it wouldn't work *now.* Find out. Get the facts. Use data. Be sure. Pilot.[15]

Move staff around. Don't be arbitrary. Look to see where skills can be better utilized or shared. Without damaging stability, you could be offering fresh perspectives.

Pull people together. Some moves can be temporary, in order to facilitate a special work team or task force as they collaborate on a special project. Be sure the teams you build are vertical, when possible. Any opportunity to bring management or supervisors together to work closely with line staff can help strengthen the fact that they're all working toward the same goals.

Listen to your young people. Energy, enthusiasm, and a wealth of new ideas come with new staff. Don't allow your longtime staff to feel threatened, but, rather, encourage all to value and respect one another.

No one should inherit a position. If your goal is to consistently spark change and innovation, don't limit your library's options. Always look far and wide for the *best* candidate and don't ever settle for the *easiest.*

Reward and recognize your change leaders. Staff should see that originality, innovation, and initiative get rewarded with everything from open praise to promotion. You can then answer "Why didn't I get promoted" with "Look around you at those who have. That's what you need to do!"[17]

Don't settle for just *comfortable with innovation.* To really effect change as an ongoing, day-to-day excitement and opportunity, it has to become second nature to your organization. Then all your planning, all your ideas, and all your staff's energy can really be put to use—through action!

Suggested Reading

Casey, Michael E., and Laura C. Savastinuk. *Library 2.0: A Guide to Participatory Library Service.* Medford, NJ: Information Today, 2007.

WORKSHEET

1. **How are ideas** brought forth in your library? Describe the process. List the five most recent ideas that have been brought to you by staff. Were they acted upon? How was that initiative celebrated?

2. **Name the "change** leaders" at your library. What qualities do they have that make them so? List the qualities, then note ways you could encourage other staff members to learn them.

3. **When was the** last time staff members were given the opportunity to work in other locations or even buildings within your library? Think about at least one opportunity existing right now where someone's particular talents or attitude would benefit another area in need of them. How might you go about initiating that move?

4. **Draft a sample** e-mail you might write to your staff explaining why you're doing the transfer in question 3. Be sure to include objectives, benefits, and an acknowledgment of the reservations they will likely have. Now, can you do it?

5. **Think of the** biggest issue facing your staff today. For example, are you facing budget cuts and need to make sweeping spending adjustments? Plan how you might pull together a special task force to meet this challenge with innovations and fresh ideas. List who might be on that task force (thinking vertically and being sure to include your change leaders). Draft what charge you would give them and how you would support their work. Now, take action. Create the task force!

Leadership

WEEK FOUR | LEADERS KNOW WHO THEY ARE

All these years, I've thought that I was following the sage advice of one of my writing heroes, humorist Erma Bombeck. "Luck," I heard she once said, "is the meeting of preparation and opportunity." The fact that I've since learned that Seneca, a first-century Roman philosopher, probably said it first doesn't matter. Erma was still smart enough to repeat it.

You're the boss now, and all the preparation you've put into your career, coupled with all the opportunities you've either chased or earned or maybe just luckily found, have put you where you need to be. How did you prepare? That's all the hard work done in school and in workshops and in training programs like this one. That's all the jobs you've ever had and includes all the lessons you've learned doing everything from waiting tables to mowing lawns to, now, management. That's all the advice you've been smart enough to listen to—or ignore—and that you've chosen wisely between the two. Every time you find yourself sitting on the praying side of an interview table, you've *prepared* to be there. Maybe you didn't even know it, but you've probably always been a leader.

Leaders know who they are. And right about now, you might be starting to panic a bit because you can't quite remember everything you've learned that's gotten you this far. Relax. This is just another opportunity! You have a chance now to *trust* your leadership abilities, so you can focus your energy on the job at hand.

If you need to be convinced of that, then maybe it's time to back up a bit and consider the bigger picture of leadership. When you need some extra confidence in yourself, when the complexities you are facing seem daunting, you can find yourself in the description of leadership and move forward with more self-assurance.

Leaders appreciate who they are. Don't waste your time or energy trying to act like someone else. Learn from others but be unique.

PREPARING to BE a LEADER

Intentionally or by instinct, most leaders have been likely to

1. *Be authentic.* The way they behave and think is completely aligned with—indeed led by—their deepest personal beliefs and values. Juggling being true to themselves and being true to their organization is what the best leaders do best.
2. *Have high emotional intelligence.* They are aware of their own emotions and they manage them effectively. They are aware of others' emotions. Recognizing both, they help people get better at what they do best.
3. *Paint a vision.* They inspire in others the trust and belief that they can lead them toward the vision. Their visions are compelling, inspiring, clear, and meaningful. They show people what the future will be like.
4. *Be passionate.* Their enthusiasm is dynamic and constant. Leaders are not easily fazed by setbacks. Their excitement is infectious.
5. *Be humble.* They are always more focused on the success of the organization and on others than on themselves. They build teams with great synergy that can—and do—succeed without them. As the founder of Taoism, Lao Tzu, said, "The leader is best when people are hardly aware of his existence."[18]

Leaders have a positive attitude. A definition of *attitude* can be how you habitually think and react. Don't be shaken by life and don't ever dwell on the negative.

Leaders believe in themselves. You know you can conquer anything, right? There is nothing wrong with regarding oneself highly. Confidence begins with you.

For leaders, change is a way of life. Rather than fear change, leaders initiate it. They act, rather than react.

Leaders plan ahead. If you know where you're going and how you're going to get there, others will see that and follow.

DEVELOPING YOUR LEADERSHIP STYLE

- *Build relationships.* When you care about people, they will care about you.
- *Stop networking.* You spend so much time trading cards and sucking up to people higher up that you don't even like. It doesn't help your leadership or your career. Stop doing it. Like I said, it is all about relationships. Get to know people who you like and, guess what, who like you too. This way you are both invested in each other. Doesn't that make more sense than talking to a seventy-year-old VP who could care less about you?
- *Create an inner circle.* This is your opportunity to develop your team.
- *Be positive.* How about instead of always pointing out the flaws, you are the first to say "thank you" or "good job." This builds in positive reinforcement and gets people feeling appreciated. You will stand out in the crowd.
- *Play to your strengths.* Know what you are good at and do it often.
- *Cover your weaknesses.* First you need to know where you are weak, and then cover those weaknesses. Not by hiding them but by surrounding yourself with people who have strengths in the areas where you are weak.
- *Commit to a career and not a company (or library).* Decide what your career is and work on it. No longer do you have to hope the VP will die so you can have his job; you will get calls hoping you will come over . . . because of your experience, drive, and leadership.
- *Treat people as people.* If you do not like people, then don't be a leader.
- *Find a work/life balance.* Life is too short if you live at your job. You set your career and boundaries. Create a balance no matter what. You will not regret it, and it will make you even stronger at work.
- *Be yourself.* Being who you are makes you different, and different is what every employer wants.[19]

Leaders build relationships with quality people. You won't win everyone over and you don't need to. Nurture relationships with people who can help you grow and learn.

Leaders are optimists. Even in the worst situations, you can always learn something.

Leaders build up other people. Empowering others to become better employees, citizens, and colleagues is a sure sign of greatness.[20]

You're the boss, so you're a leader. You see yourself in these descriptions. Don't get lost in the magnitude of the job; instead, be strengthened by the qualities you bring to it. So be confident and get busy. Remember: "To accomplish what we have never done, we have to do things we've never attempted."[21]

You are nearing the end of this development year, and it's almost time to begin considering your future. During the last month of this process, you're going to be doing some specific planning to see what your future might include. In order to frame that future, you need to define your own *hedgehog* drivers. As an example, here are mine.

My *passion* is to see libraries succeed in the twenty-first century—in their new role. What I *do better than anything else* is to train and teach. My *resource* is people. I'll work with staff in whatever way I can, reaching people in any and all positions, to move them forward, so they bring their libraries along with them. I will measure all opportunities that come my way against these principles. That will mean I'll say "no" to some. That will mean I'll work harder to seek out others.

How about you? You are the boss. You are already a leader. How will your leadership show through the rest of your career?

WORKSHEET

1. **Describe the passion** that drives your career.

2. **Next, consider at** what professional skills you excel.

3. **Finally, what is** your resource? Is it materials, as in your collection? Is it money, as in the contracts you negotiate for your library or the vendor relationships you build? Is it your staff? Your community network?

4. **You have your** *hedgehog concept* described clearly now. How will you use it? List the five primary, professional career goals at which you can work next. Next month, you'll be spending some time creating a plan to achieve each and every one of them.

Your Future

WEEK ONE DAMAGE CONTROL

Before this yearlong development project ends, you have to know something important. You're going to make mistakes. You'll tell others on your watch that they can have bad days and then you yourself will have them too. There's no escaping it. You'll encourage supervisors to always be appreciative in their mentoring, and then you'll come down on someone. You'll expect others to make good, thoughtful decisions and then you'll make a bad one. All of this, everything you've read and learned and will continue to learn, won't work every day. But that's okay, for two reasons. The first is that we're all just human, and the second is that we can apply *damage control* and then try again.

When she came into her manager's office, the department head was distraught. Everything was a mess and, at least in her opinion, it was all her fault. The story went like this. When she'd first hired her good friend as a librarian in the department, she figured it would be easy. They got along really well, continued to confide in one another like they'd done for years, and were even able to go out together once in a while, while keeping their relationship at work professional. Or, at least, that's what she'd hoped.

Lately, though, her friend had been coming in late habitually and not getting her work done, and the rest of the department was suffering and, now, claiming favoritism. The manager asked her if she'd been addressing and documenting the tardiness and other performance problems. No, she answered uncomfortably, she hadn't. It had seemed too weird to do that. They'd known each other for twenty years. After all, other than recently, the librarian was great at reference and storytelling. This morning, though, the union rep had called her and asked for a meeting, telling her a class action grievance was being filed against her for allowing the problems to go on uncorrected.

DAMAGE CONTROL EMPHASIS

Don't Focus on:

- Blame-storming instead of brainstorming
- Scorekeeping
- Long memories

Do Focus on:

- Action
- Quick recovery
- Coping
- (Later) accountability for impact on results and people[1]

MISTAKES ARE INEVITABLE—WITHOUT THEM, SUCCESS IS NOT

Jack Ricchiuto points to several "successes" that took some practice:

- In a survey of baseball greats, we find that the top 10 hitters took an average of 54 swings for each home run.
- The *Star Wars* movie concept was rejected by twelve Hollywood studios before it was finally accepted.
- Post-it notes failed in all four of its first market tests.
- In 1962, Decca Records told the Beatles that groups with guitars were on their way "out."[3]

You're probably wondering why, after almost an entire year working through this development book, you are just now getting to the *basics*, like making mistakes. It's because some things will recur in almost every situation you'll encounter. This story is just one example of a basic truth you'll need to face—*you're going to make mistakes.* It doesn't matter how much you read or how hard you study or what you're able to learn, you simply cannot be a great boss all the time. And that's just the first basic truth we'll deal with in this, your final month.

So what happened?

The manager in this situation, who was one of the best I've ever known, had just two words for her department head: *damage control.* When you make a mistake or act on a poor judgment or just plain miss something, think *first* of your primary responsibility—the library—and take steps to make sure to minimize the consequences however you can. Who might be hurt by your error? Can you intervene to limit the damage? What might be the repercussions down the road? How can you ameliorate them? Spending time, especially at the beginning of a problem, wringing your hands or berating yourself doesn't protect your library or your staff from additional damage. You need to do that first.

As author John Miller has stated, "Ownership is a commitment of the head, heart and hands to fix the problem and never again affix the blame."[2]

Later, after the dust has settled, there will be plenty of time for review and for finding that one thing (at least) that you can learn from a bad experience, which will make you a better boss going forward.

When you're the boss, the best thing you can do is to close your car door in the morning and walk toward the building thinking, "I can handle whatever happens today. I can improve it or support it or, if necessary, fix it." Because that's what others will need you to do. What you should never walk into work thinking is, "I've learned all I need to know. I'm perfect and nothing will go wrong today. If it does, I'll be certain that it's someone else's fault." Those bosses are yesterday's bosses, literally and figuratively!

A very wise pediatrician once advised new parents that if their child didn't have at least one bump or bruise or Band-Aid on him at all times, they were being overprotective parents, which is potentially even more damaging. The same can be said of organizations. If someone on your staff doesn't make a mistake with consistent regularity, then you're not all trying enough new ideas or taking enough risks. Just like debt, risks are to be well managed—not avoided.

Another factor that will assure your staff that you're going to help with a crisis and not just react to it is memory. Yours. Imagine how difficult it would be for you to do your job if every single mistake you've ever made was brought up and reviewed at the beginning of each staff meeting. What kind of confidence and trust would that build between you and your staff? Everyone needs the chance to start over every day.

To live and learn, as the saying goes. At one library, when kids (or adults) become over-the-top disruptive or rude or even antagonistic, they're sent home *for the day*. Staff guards escorting them out of the building, with the kids grumbling all the way, dismiss them with a call of "See you tomorrow." They can come back and try again.

Most libraries operate that way, since it would be unreasonable to assume that everyone who acts out will be banned for life. Staff deserve that same opportunity. Don't grudgingly harbor ill will from transgressions gone by. Give everyone, including yourself, a chance to show what they've learned and how they've grown.

How can a great boss be so open and accepting of mistakes? Perhaps that's the greatest secret of all. It's called kindness. While you may not have read it in the job description, that's the element of your personality—the most basic component—that's going to make a success out of all you do. "Kindness and leadership," Baker and O'Malley suggest, "are complementary and . . . this combination *specifically* gives a leader a crucial edge."[4]

Be as ready for failure as you are for success because you and your staff will face both. And that's a basic fact.

Suggested Reading

Baker, William F., and Michael O'Malley. *Leading with Kindness: How Good People Consistently Get Superior Results*. New York: American Management Association, 2008.

WORKSHEET

1. **Think of the** most recent time a member of your staff has reported to you a mistake she has made. List as much about your initial reaction as you can recall and then consider it against the "damage control first" concept.

2. **How could your** reaction to the incident in the first question have been better? How would you react now, if you had another chance?

3. **Think of the** most upsetting mistake you have made recently. List as many things as you can think of that you can learn from the experience.

4. **If they were** asked, what might your staff say is your normal reaction when something goes wrong? If you can't honestly answer this yourself, go ask some of them.

5. **From the answers** in the question above, how do you think you can be better prepared, each and every day, to react well to mistakes? What *specifically* can you start doing today?

Your Future

WEEK TWO | HABITS AND CRUTCHES

One difference between a habit and a crutch is that we'll usually admit to one and not the other. Crutches, in other words, are habits gone bad. Crutches are excuses not to do something, like be a great boss. They sound good, but nobody believes them. It's easy to get caught in their grip and let everything else you've learned fall away. Don't do it.

From every boss's office, cries of helplessness can be heard as leaders plead the many reasons why they can't be *great.* If there was a "Top Ten List" of those reasons (and there probably is, somewhere), these would probably be the top three: (1) "There isn't enough time" (crutch); (2) "You never sent that to me" (crutch), also known as "I did not lose it! My desk may be a mess, but I know where everything is" (lie and crutch); and (3) "I'm too stressed" (biggest crutch, since bosses should be able to handle stress).

You are near the end of this important development year. You've got a lot of work ahead of you. Last week, you faced what is perhaps the biggest barrier to success when you admitted that you are going to make mistakes. You'll face them, admit them, limit the damage, learn from them, and move on. Now it's time to take a look at these other *big* three crutches that could be your speed bumps to achievement—and get them out of your way as well.

THERE ISN'T ENOUGH TIME

Correct me if I'm wrong. When you began this workbook almost one year ago and you first read that you'd have to devote one full hour a week to it, you thought that would be impossible, right? Be honest. You thought it couldn't be done, right? But you did it. You decided that your own growth and development was worth the time it would take to keep a one-hour slot clear, so you accomplished that.

Let's consider this time question. No one would argue that you aren't busy. We all are. But, like most bosses, you probably work more reactively than proactively, which can be a big waste of your time. Your habit is to flit from topic to topic, putting out fires as you go. Or worse yet, you may be in the habit of personally reacting and responding to each and every crisis that comes along. Do you jump in and "fix" problems, rather than stand back, hold your breath, count to ten, and let your team handle them? If you do that, then you're wasting their time *and* yours. Given this scenario, you may even think you don't have the time to be great, and if you hang on to these crutches, you'll be right. No one has the time to do the job of ten people! No kidding. The very best way to start correcting these bad habits is to *trust others.*

Try just doing your own job for a while. Whether you've got one other person to help run the place or a hundred, trust them. Use *your* time wisely. Let them use *their* time to do their jobs. Prioritize. You should be plotting how you will be spending your time by the year, by the month, by the week, and then morning by morning. Not by the ringing phone or the blinking e-mail in front of you.

Do you have an annual planning calendar? Do you keep to-do lists? These are not the tools of the weak-minded; these are the tools of the wise. How many bosses have you had who can't seem to stay focused on an issue all the way through to resolution? Think about the impact that had on the rest of the staff. Don't go back over issues and back and back. If you don't bring time management skills to your job, then do something about that and learn them. Your staff and your library need every minute you contribute to your job to mean something. Lose the crutch of blaming time and, instead, make the best of every moment. One way to keep better control over what you really do every day is to journal.

Your time is important. First, decide not to waste it and then, while you're at it, decide not to lose it either. Scott Sheperd warns us "it is critical that we not miss our lives as we move through them."[5] As this is being written, 2010 has just begun. It seems that it was just a moment ago that the world was heralding the start of the twenty-first century, proving that even a decade can pass by in the blink of an eye. I don't know about you, but that decade was part of my career! I can only hope I used that time wisely.

JOURNALING for GROWTH

Human Resources Coordinator Laurie Marotta suggests that we need to "stand back, take a good look at ourselves and assess our own growth and opportunities . . . In order to capture your development and be able to talk about it, you should be keeping a record of your experiences." While you're learning to master your workplace, skills, and time, her advice is to "track completed assignments, work experiences, projects, learning opportunities and new skills."[6] How to do this? Try keeping a journal. Here are some practical suggestions on how to get started journaling.

1. Find a journal you can carry with you. Pick a small notebook or PDA that fits in your purse or briefcase. You'll never know when you're going to get a minute to write. You could be waiting on hold for someone or passing a few minutes in between meetings. You're only going to need a couple minutes a day.
2. Write for yourself—simply and without being perfect. Don't worry about how neat your entry looks or whether or not the grammar and punctuation are perfect. You're writing notes to yourself, and all you need to do is make enough sense so that you'll understand when you reread it later.
3. Be honest. It's doubtful the *New York Times* will ever discover and publish your journal, so be honest about what you're thinking and feeling.
4. Pick a time of the day for writing—and stick with it.
5. Set goals and check up on yourself. If you say you'll do (something) in the coming month, go thirty pages ahead and write in "Have I improved?" It's easy for all of us to forget what we're really trying to do.
6. If you need to, start small. If writing, even a little, each day you work is too daunting a task for you in the beginning, just keep a simple list of projects completed or situations handled and enter it weekly. Your journaling can grow as you can increase the time you spend working on it.[7]

YOU NEVER SENT THAT TO ME

To tackle the next crutch, look at your desk. Look all around your desk, at everything else in your office. If you're really bad at this, look *under* your desk (in one employee's office, I once found fourteen dirty coffee cups and several bank statements stored there). Quick! Where is that memo you need to respond to regarding next year's budget? Can you find it? Where is that evaluation you're supposed to be filling out and, more important, where is the one from last year, so you can see if goals were met? After all the time you've spent over the past several months considering important, weighty matters like budgeting and personnel, it might seem superfluous to pause now to consider neatness and organization—but if you can't immediately find either document, then these are *key* to your success in moving forward.

While it's true that Albert Einstein once said, "If a cluttered desk signs a cluttered mind, of what, then, is an empty desk a sign?"[8] it's possible that no one wrote down what might have come next—where the common ground should be. You need to have an organized desk. An organized mind. Organized work.

It sounds simple, but the best way to ditch the "I lost it, I can't find it, and you never gave it to me" crutch is to *get organized, once and for all!* Talk to someone who manages their work well. Read a book about organization. Take a course in productivity. These can often sound trite: "Clear Your Desk," or "Get Organized," or "Get More Done." But no other habit can be more valuable to a great boss than having mastery of her domain! While you can't let your job control your time, as we've discussed, you can't let sloppiness control it either. Learn simple tricks that can change your life. Handle everything only once. Keep all your notes in one place. Use a labeler. Sound trivial? It isn't. And it won't only affect you. As a role model for your staff, there's no better example to set than as someone who controls their work—not the other way around.

Think about it. What was your reaction the last time someone interrupted you at a critical point in your work to ask, "Do you have a minute?" Hopefully you smiled, pushed your papers away, and invited them to sit and share their problems. You knew what you absolutely had to get done that day, how much time each action would take, and where everything you needed to use was located. You had the time to do your *real* job. Counseling. Mentoring. Offering support. Problem solving. You had time to offer them *you*.

I'M TOO STRESSED

The last crutch you need to lose is the ever-popular "I'm too stressed" excuse, which can cripple even the best intentioned among us. Some bosses blame everything they do wrong (or don't do at all) on stress. Arrgggh! You can't think straight! You're so mad! It's so frustrating! You're buckling under all the stress! This job is hard! Everyone's blaming you for everything! Remember, "when employees are unhappy, they blame the boss."[9] That can be stressful, right? Wrong, or at least, it doesn't have to be.

It can also help to remember that "stress doesn't kill us, we commit suicide with it."[10]

Claiming that you can't handle the stress that comes from being the boss is another crutch, rut, or bad habit you must avoid. Guess what? Those other staffers around you—you know, the ones making half your salary and working just as hard—don't want to hear you complain about your stress. And they *really* don't want to operate under the impression that you can't handle the job. After all, if you can't, why should they? And the people who are paying you that extra money, that lifts your responsibilities over those of everyone else, they don't want to hear it either.

A lot of the blame for this attitude has to do with your desire for perfection. You've always had it. Admit it. That's why you became a librarian. You've wanted to keep everything in order, well managed, and lined up, right down to the hundred thousandth of the call number, right? Well, guess what? There isn't any way to make the boss's job less complex or to keep it that well managed, day to day. But there is a way to improve how you *deal* with the challenges you'll be handed—and it's called stress management or *patience*. When the really tough problems come your way—and they will because that's the direction they're supposed to go—try reflecting instead of just reacting. Just as we learned as children, take a breath (again) and stop and think before you speak or act. You're going to find that the more you manage your time, work, and stress, the easier this formidable step will become.

Your staff want to have confidence in you. They want and need to know that you're at the helm, you're in charge, and you can handle it. A wise manager once told me that if you don't feel in control, then fake it. This isn't a bad thing because, eventually, you will have it all handled. If you have to, simply stall at moments of high pressure. Inspire the confidence that you will get back to everyone with the right answer, and then go somewhere and think. Tell staff you'll get back to them. Say you'll give it some thought and let them know. What you say will show how you're controlling their—and your—stress. And that's what they look to you for. Control. Management. Leadership. So choose your actions and your words carefully!

Control your job's stress, rather than the other way around, and you'll have overcome yet another hurdle to your success.

You now have some of the biggest hurdles you'll face out of your way, or at least on the road to being well managed. You know you'll make mistakes and that you can repair the damage and move on. You know now that you *can* control your time, your work, and your stress. So, in place of these, what *good* habits should you be developing as you become a great boss?

The practical habits are clear and you've spent the last year developing them. Inside, though, you'll need to continue to grow as a leader and, for that, Baker and O'Malley offer the best advice I've found. Always, every day, in every interaction, build relationships by demonstrating "compassion, integrity, gratitude, authenticity, humility and humor."[11]

It's on these great crutches that your professional success can be built.

Suggested Reading

Sheperd, Scott. *Who's in Charge? Attacking the Stress Myth.* Highland City, FL: Rainbow Books, 2003.

DON'T GIVE STRESS a VOICE

- *Try difficult instead of terrible.* The next time you are having a tough time, try using the word *difficult* to describe it. If I came up to you and said, "Hey, I've got a couple of jobs for you to choose from—one's difficult and one's terrible—what do you think?" would you possibly think there is a difference? Let's face it; *terrible* brings things to mind that *difficult* doesn't.
- *Question carefully.* When facing stress, if your next reaction is "Why me?" you are really asking for trouble. Try "Who knows anything about this?" or "What are my options?" or "Who will be honest with me?" If you ask questions that keep you stuck in bad places, then you probably will stay stuck for quite a while.
- *Life offers opportunities—live your life.* There are two sides to every situation—sunlight and shadow, sleeping and awake, light and dark, life and death. You can live your life in fear of pain, disappointment, and loss. You can spend all your time "stressed out" and being a victim. You can miss all kinds of opportunities, or you can enter into life and take the good *and* the bad.
- *Use your personal power.* The woe-is-me approach doesn't allow a person to go anywhere but down. Other, more positive choices give a person a direction, a sense of his or her own power.
- *Neutral isn't a choice.* Negative people don't pull positive people down. They go willingly. You are either growing or dying. As they said in the 1960s, if you're not part of the solution, you're part of the problem. There is no neutral in life.
- *Don't hang out with dead people.* I have been in many organizations that have a lot of dead people working for them. It might be forty years before they fall down and make it official, but they are dead. Don't hang out with dead people. And for sure don't hand over your mind and spirit to them.[12]

WORKSHEET

1. **List at least** ten things that you don't have time to do this week but that you wish you did. Put a checkmark next to the three that you *most* wish you could do.

2. **List at least** ten things that you *do have time to do* this week. Pick three that you don't *really* need (or want) to do and put a checkmark next to them. Now, switch them out with the three in question 1.

3. **Time yourself with** this one. See if you can find these three things, in under one minute: the agenda from your last staff meeting, the library's budget from two years ago, and a list of all staff phone numbers. Go! If you can, then you keep your work area well organized and managed—keep it up. If you can't, then go find a book on work-place organization, buy a label gun, get some blank folders, and get to work. (Also, add to your career strategy plan, for the coming year, your attending at least one "Get Organized" workshop!)

4. **What are the** five things you do most frequently to deal with stress?

5. **How well do** they work? List the most recent five things you did or said that you wish you could take back, but you were *stressed!*

Always seek balance in your work and life. No one but you can tell if stress is getting to you (unless you've done something terribly overt and, if so, you've probably been guided toward some *required* help; hopefully, that's not the case). Look over your answers, and if you need more help managing your stress, look around to find some. (If your library has an employee support contract, use it! Counselors available through these programs are often very well versed in helping manage workplace challenges. They can help you more than you'd ever expect and they can put you on the right path for continued success.)

Your Future

WEEK THREE | A STRATEGIC CAREER

What's your plan for the rest of the day? What's on the slate?

You've got one hour to devote to your workbook, and then what, lunch? Do you have other meetings this afternoon? What about tomorrow? The next day? What's the one biggest thing you hope to accomplish at work, at least before the week is over? How about sometime this year? Do you dread that traditional interview question, "Where do you see yourself in five years?" because you have no clue how to answer it? What has to happen for you to be successful? What can you do to help that happen?

Lots of questions and really just one answer. What we're talking about here is having a strategy. Chances are, your library has a strategic plan someplace. Look around. You looked at it earlier this year for a previous assignment. Now, where did it get to? Top shelf, maybe, way back, behind the microwave oatmeal packets? If you're lucky, your library not only *has* a plan, it uses it. With a plan, success is more likely since, after all, if you don't know where you're going, how will you know when you get there? Or, as author John Miller points out, "If we don't ask what we can do or make or achieve or build, then we won't do or make or achieve or build. It's just that simple. Only through action is anything accomplished."[13]

And action needs to be planned.

The same can and should be said about your career. Do you have any strategy at all? Let me tell you something you may not believe. Even a thirty-year career will go by in the blink of an eye. You're going to open your eyes one day and you'll be at your own retirement party, and when they hand you the mike, what do you want to be able to say? Will it be "As soon as this one job I've got my eye on opens up, I think my next career step will be to apply for it." Or will you say, "I may not have gotten every single job I wanted, but I did reach the important goals I'd set along the way, so that, in my career, I've been able to accomplish what I think are the really important things" . . . And then you fill in the blanks.

In order to be able to say that, you are going to need a strategy.

Most new bosses are expected to hit the ground running when they start a new job. Usually, you're filling a staffing hole that, while left open, has resulted in a lot of work going undone. Whether you're prepared or not, you're often expected to "get up to speed quickly. Reorient the organization. Produce results in a short time frame. Right wrongs. Repair damage. Restructure. Refocus. Recharge the organization" (or your corner of it).[14] No small order.

This development year is almost over, and completing this workbook has, hopefully, been a great jumping-off point for you. Now, though, it's time to begin looking at the next years of your career, which are just around the corner.

Even when you began working through this program, you hopefully were looking for development in an area of need, based on your skills, as well as in an area that will help move you closer to where you want to be. Year by year, that won't likely change. It's your *mission,* after all, that leads you to take one job, pass up others, and continue trying to learn along the way. When you think about your mission, you should be seeing the big picture of what you want to do in your working *lifetime.* That's what you're going to want to talk about, at that retirement party. You're not going to jump from wanting to make an impact in public libraries to wanting to become a concert pianist—probably. While, surely, your mission can bend a bit, it should unwaveringly move you closer, year by year, to the person you want to become and to achieving the professional contribution you want to make.

One of the most damaging things that can happen to any boss's productivity, initiative, and, most basically, attitude is to allow herself to move into a *mission ignore* phase of her career. Unlike the perhaps better-known issue of *mission creep,* where targets are constantly changing, this individual shortcoming is usually brought about by a combination of lack of attention, frustration, and even fear of the unknown.

It's easier not to apply for that big promotion than to go for it. Should you give it a shot? Or should you not? To answer that question wisely and still stay on track, you're going to need a plan. Remember, "if someone said they were going to achieve something that will make a difference in their world without goals and plans, we would consider them immature or insane."[15] There's a reason for that.

Throughout your career, you'll likely be faced with many decisions, with many turns in the road, around which you'll have to navigate, and with many roadblocks at worst or speed bumps at best that will get in your way. There's an easy way to stay on course when this happens. Have a career strategy and stick to it.

Even if you're in the last few years of your career, don't forget what you're really trying to do. Don't just live to the end.

Always know your career's mission. Clarify it. Post it on your printer or carry it in your purse or wallet. Look at it every five years or so and make sure it still makes you smile or intrigues you. From that mission, make all of your other career decisions. Start each year by naming at least two or three accomplishments you want to achieve before New Year's Eve. Then spend some time with those ideas. Spend enough time that you're excited about them. Stop before you get jaded by them.

Make a plan to achieve the goals you've set. Write it down somewhere. Show it to someone! There are probably several smaller steps you can take to help you achieve the accomplishments you've identified. Every three months or so, do a spot check to see where you are in your progress. Then, when the year wraps up, find out *why* you fell short in some areas. If those goals are still important, learn from the previous year and make the next one better.

Your goals can and likely should change a bit from year to year, depending both on what's available for you to do and what's happening in the professional marketplace and in your own library. Did your boss change? Then perhaps you'll have to rearrange your goals. That's okay, though, as long as you stick to your overall career mission. For example, for someone who started as a library page twenty-plus years ago and whose mission is to make a significant contribution to helping train others to excel in libraries, it's okay to shift goals one year from *teach more classes* to *provide transitional support for the new boss.* That person is still training and helping others to develop, right? She's just taking a little different tack until the ground under her firms up enough again to branch out.

So at the end of each year, when you're cleaning out your files, maybe writing evaluations or just setting up your new calendar, add this one critical step in your own strategic career development . . . *set your professional goals for the coming year again.* Pull out your career mission statement and check to see that your goals are still aligned correctly, and then you can start making plans to implement your strategy with all the options available to you today—and tomorrow. Don't forget to drill down past the goals to the action you plan to take. The words you use don't matter (goals, objectives, initiatives) but the concepts will be the same.

Know where you're going. Know what you have to accomplish in order to get there. Know the steps you can take to achieve those accomplishments.

Don't forget to check in at least quarterly throughout the year. Whether you can tell statistically that you've accomplished something or whether you need a much less empirical measurement to be sure, you have to stop and check. Measure where you are. Measure your progress and celebrate your successes all along the way. In that way, year 10 will look better than year 5, and year 20 will feel great compared to year 12 . . . and so on, right up to your carefully calculated last day. Planner Joe Matthews reminds us that "what gets measured gets done."[16]

And one more thing, one very important thing to remember about this plan: be prepared to amend it whenever necessary. "Change is good until it happens to you," reorganization survivor Cheryl Teresi tells us.[17] She also offers a warning that "in the same way a daily commute becomes automatic, it is possible to drift through uninterrupted routine without effort or reflection . . . When you hear the news that your work situation will be changing or reorganizing, stay positive . . . Who knew? What's next? New opportunities are always within reach."[18]

Just as it is critical to *have* a strategy for your career, it is equally imperative that you allow for adjustments to it—and improvements—and *surprises* along the way. To remain poised for just such opportunities, every time you reconsider the strategy you've devised for yourself, remember to ask this one very important question—and listen for the answer.

YOUR PROFESSIONAL SWOT

In any planning process, there is an initial need to identify strengths, weaknesses, opportunities, and threats. When considering a person, rather than an organization, there's a unique way to approach this. Try considering it this way:

- *For strengths:* What was the best day at work you've had in the last three months? What were you doing? Why did you enjoy it so much?
- *For weaknesses:* What was your worst day at work in the last three months? What were you doing? Why did it grate on you so much?
- *For triggers (or possible opportunities for growth):* What was the best relationship with a manager you've ever had? What made it work so well? What was the best praise or recognition you've ever received? What made it so good?[19]
- *For threats to your growth:* Consider the opposite of the triggers.

"What *else* can I do to rise above my circumstances and achieve the results I desire?"[20]

There's always going to be something else!

Suggested Reading

Buckingham, Marcus. *The One Thing You Need to Know . . . about Great Managing, Great Leading, and Sustained Individual Success.* New York: Free Press, 2005.

WORKSHEET

1. **At the end** of your career, when you open the newspaper to read the story someone has written about what you did, what do you want the first paragraph to say that you accomplished? *That's your mission.* Write the first paragraph of your professional legacy below.

____

____

2. **Between now and** when you take this workbook out again in one year to review it, what three major accomplishments do you hope to achieve that will move you closer to achieving your mission? List them here. *These are your (current) goals.*

   Goal 1: ____

   Goal 2: ____

   Goal 3: ____

3. **In order to** achieve each of your three goals, consider each one individually and decide what has to happen and how you will know when it has. For each goal, list at least two individual achievements. *These are your objectives and their measurements.*

   For Goal 1 ____

   Objective 1 ____

   ____

   How you'll know when you've achieved it: ____

   ____

   Objective 2 ____

   ____

   How you'll know when you've achieved it: ____

   ____

   For Goal 2 ____

   Objective 1 ____

   ____

   How you'll know when you've achieved it: ____

   ____

   Objective 2 ____

   ____

   How you'll know when you've achieved it: ____

   ____

For Goal 3 ____

____

Objective 1 ____

____

How you'll know when you've achieved it: ______________________________

____

Objective 2 ____

____

How you'll know when you've achieved it: ______________________________

____

4. **In order to** achieve objectives, you have to take action. During this year, what can you do in order to successfully reach your stated objectives? What will at least two specific action plans be for each objective?

For Goal 1, Objective 1

(Action step) ____

(Action step) ____

For Goal 1, Objective 2

(Action step) ____

(Action step) ____

For Goal 2, Objective 1

(Action step) ____

(Action step) ____

For Goal 2, Objective 2

(Action step) ____

(Action step) ____

For Goal 3, Objective 1

(Action step) ____

(Action step) ____

For Goal 3, Objective 2

(Action step) ____

(Action step) ____

5. **Mark on your** calendar to return to this worksheet in three to six months. After evaluating the progress you made and what, if anything, got in your way, update the plan, if necessary, so you can continue moving forward.

Your Future

WEEK FOUR | BACK TO ATTITUDE

In the end, it all comes back to attitude.

You've got to want to always keep learning. You've got to want to keep getting better. You must never become one of those horrid bosses who think they know everything. Who thinks they're always right. Who thinks they have nothing else to learn, because the most recent promotion also altered their professional status to perfect. They think they're better, smarter, faster, and more important than the average bear—you know the type. *Not* a great boss to have or to be!

Have the right attitude. You had it at the beginning of this project; just be sure to keep it! Have an attitude of humility, an attitude of appreciation for the opportunities you've been given, and an attitude of perpetual eagerness to never stop learning.

Whenever you are unsure of what type of boss you want to be, just think back to what type of boss you want to *have.*

How, practically, can you keep the right attitude? Authors Kouzes and Posner suggest, logically, that it all comes down to what we do. To our actions. "Leadership is not a spectator sport," they explain. "Leaders do not sit in the stands and watch. Hero myths aside, neither are leaders in the game substituting for the players. Leaders coach. They show others how to behave."[21]

Here are some specific actions they suggest that can help you establish and *perpetuate* the right attitude, as you and your career move forward:

Challenge the process—be a pioneer. Innovate, experiment, and explore ways to improve the organization. Treat mistakes as learning experiences.

Inspire a shared vision—envision the future with a positive and hopeful outlook.

Enable others to act—infuse mutual trust and collaborative goals that ensure your staff feel strong and capable.

Model the way—be clear in your values and beliefs and behave consistently.

Encourage the heart—celebrate achievements and build pride.[22]

So here you are. Ready to try and launch a continually improving career that will make you a great boss? Know yourself. It's not enough to just know the job. In order to truly prepare for a new (or existing) management role, "creating self-awareness is the first step. Reading can help, and coaching or a training program will develop recognition of personal strengths and how they contribute" to the skills you need.[23]

Even though this year is almost up, you haven't finished your new commitment to self-directed learning and development. This was just your first installment. Today you're going to design next year's workbook, so you can keep your growth and development going.

You can just keep working and you will just keep working better. You've got the system down now and have hopefully laid a strong foundation over the past year. What's next? In what area do you most need to concentrate your learning? Through this week's exercises, you'll strategically plan for your career and develop an outline for your next workbook. You can put this one together yourself and focus more specifically on your own career needs. Do the same at the end of that year too, and keep going after that.

There are a lot of learned philosophers and pundits who could close this book and underscore the messages it contains, but none could do it better than novelist, columnist, and humorist Erma Bombeck.

ATTITUDE HELPERS: KEEPING the "RIGHT" SIDE of YOUR BRAIN BUSY

Trainer Marti Peden suggests research has proven, using MRI studies, that you can improve your attitude by keeping the left, prefrontal side of your brain busy, which limits what the right, prefrontal side can do to damage your attitude. Further, she suggests that it is impossible for both sides to function simultaneously. So if you're stressed and you pick something from the left column to focus on, you'll block out the damaging right side.

LEFT PREFRONTAL ACTIONS	RIGHT PREFRONTAL ACTIONS
Music	Anxiousness
Prayer	Worry
Enjoying nature	Staying too busy
Exercising	Being on the go, go, go
Showing gratitude	Displaying anger
Laughing	Being frustrated[24]

"When I stand before God at the end of my life," she wrote, "I would hope that I would not have a single bit of talent left and could say 'I used everything you gave me.'"[25]

WORKSHEET

It's time to design your training plan for the coming year.

You can do it!

While this workbook has taken you on a broad tour of being *the boss,* now it's time to close in on a more specific area in which you'd like to experience some professional growth. Next year's workbook can be more closely aligned with your particular career at this moment in time. By completing this exercise, you'll have an outline for a full year's learning. If you repeat this process again and again, at the end of each year, you'll never stop getting better!

This final exercise will take you through this task step by step. Fill in the "Table of Contents" template that is attached as an appendix to this book as you read through the steps. In order to make clearer what your final product will look like, I'll provide the table of contents for my next book, *Build a Great Team,* as an example.

You can complete this exercise in just four easy steps.

1. Select the topic, area, or issue that you'd like to tackle next.

   (*Example*) **Build a Great Team**

____

____

____

____

____

____

2. Identify four primary components of this theme. In other words, in order to really excel at your topic, what four primary concepts should you completely understand and master?

   (*Example*) **Build a Great Team**

____

____

____

____

____

____

TABLE OF CONTENTS

1. Building the Team
2. Directing the Team
3. Strengthening the Team
4. Growing Teams

3. Next, look at each of the four components individually and, for each, answer these three questions. What are the basics you need to know? What's new or innovative regarding this topic? What challenge(s) does it pose?

(*Example*) **Build a Great Team**

TABLE OF CONTENTS

Building the Team

Basics: Staffing

Innovations: Shared Leadership

Challenges: Generation Gaps

Directing the Team

Basics: Planning

Innovations: Networking

Challenges: Skill Blending

Strengthening the Team

Basics: Communication

Innovations: Mentoring

Challenges: Change Culture

Growing Teams

Basics: The Charge

Innovations: Cross-Industry

Challenges: Marketing and Results

These twelve individual concepts will become the headings for each month of this yearlong development plan.

4. You should now have filled in your entire table of contents, except for identifying the weekly topics. Your training outline is almost complete. You need to complete just that one more step. Spend some time considering each monthly heading and considering into what four pieces it can be broken. You will have to eliminate (or combine) some because you only have four weeks in a month. Try to settle on the four that are most critical to success in that area.

   (*Example*) **Build a Great Team**

TABLE OF CONTENTS

Week Three: Shared Creativity

Week Four: News

EIGHTH MONTH: Mentoring

Week One: Mentors

Week Two: Mentees

Week Three: Formal

Week Four: Informal

NINTH MONTH: Change Culture

Week One: Risk Taking

Week Two: Ideas

Week Three: Tests

Week Four: Confidence

Part Four: Growing Teams

TENTH MONTH: The Charge

Week One: Purpose

Week Two: What Teams Are Not

Week Three: Matching

Week Four: Reporting

ELEVENTH MONTH: Cross-Industry

Week One: Sources

Week Two: Colleagues

Week Three: Supporters

Week Four: Threats

TWELFTH MONTH: Marketing and Results

Week One: Origination

Week Two: Creation

Week Three: Progress

Week Four: Completion

5. So what do you do, once you have a completed outline for your coming year? You'll need to fill in the supporting information as you go along, as well as select (as I did) from those *favorite* articles and books you've been setting aside for years, that you've never quite found the time to review. Sort them out. See where they might fit in. Begin to organize the *content* that will support each category. While you're working throughout the year, continue to find new books, chapters, or articles to read, or talk to peers and specialists to fill in any gaps.

6. There's one more very important step you can't skip. You've got to create your homework. When you design your own exercises (and you definitely need to do this for the entire year), make them thought-provoking enough to really have you applying what you're learning to your real-life, professional world.

Then, go ahead and get started on your second year of growth and development. Week by week, month by month, you're going to bring a new year's worth of mastery in the concept area you selected. You've begun a great tradition this year of dedicating your time as much to your future as to your present. With that kind of focused learning, you'll be better able to succeed in whatever you do.

Excellence is a journey, not a target. Good luck.

APPENDIX | WORKBOOK TABLE OF CONTENTS TEMPLATE

WORKBOOK TITLE: ______________________________

SECTION ONE: ______________________________

(from Worksheet 48, Question 2)

(Basics) **First Month:** ______________________________

(from Worksheet 48, Question 3)

Issue/Week One: ______________________________
Issue/Week Two: ______________________________
Issue/Week Three: ______________________________
Issue/Week Four: ______________________________

(Innovations) **Second Month:** ______________________________

(from Worksheet 48, Question 3)

Issue/Week One: ______________________________
Issue/Week Two: ______________________________
Issue/Week Three: ______________________________
Issue/Week Four: ______________________________

(Challenges) **Third Month:** ______________________________

(from Worksheet 48, Question 3)

Issue/Week One: ______________________________
Issue/Week Two: ______________________________
Issue/Week Three: ______________________________
Issue/Week Four: ______________________________

SECTION TWO: ______________________________

(from Worksheet 48, Question 2)

(Basics) **Fourth Month:** ______________________________

(from Worksheet 48, Question 3)

Issue/Week One: ______________________________
Issue/Week Two: ______________________________
Issue/Week Three: ______________________________
Issue/Week Four: ______________________________

(Innovations) **Fifth Month:**____________________

(from Worksheet 48, Question 3)

Issue/Week One: ____________________
Issue/Week Two: ____________________
Issue/Week Three: ____________________
Issue/Week Four: ____________________

(Challenges) **Sixth Month:**____________________

(from Worksheet 48, Question 3)

Issue/Week One:____________________
Issue/Week Two: ____________________
Issue/Week Three: ____________________
Issue/Week Four: ____________________

SECTION THREE: ____________________

(from Worksheet 48, Question 2)

(Basics) **Seventh Month:**____________________

(from Worksheet 48, Question 3)

Issue/Week One: ____________________
Issue/Week Two: ____________________
Issue/Week Three: ____________________
Issue/Week Four: ____________________

(Innovations) **Eighth Month:**____________________

(from Worksheet 48, Question 3)

Issue/Week One: ____________________
Issue/Week Two: ____________________
Issue/Week Three: ____________________
Issue/Week Four: ____________________

(Challenges) **Ninth Month:**____________________

(from Worksheet 48, Question 3)

Issue/Week One: ____________________
Issue/Week Two: ____________________
Issue/Week Three: ____________________
Issue/Week Four: ____________________

SECTION FOUR: ____________________

(from Worksheet 48, Question 2)

(Basics) **Tenth Month:**____________________

(from Worksheet 48, Question 3)

Issue/Week One: ____________________
Issue/Week Two: ____________________
Issue/Week Three: ____________________
Issue/Week Four: ____________________

(Innovations) **Eleventh Month:**____________________

(from Worksheet 48, Question 3)

Issue/Week One: ____________________
Issue/Week Two: ____________________
Issue/Week Three: ____________________
Issue/Week Four: ____________________

(Challenges) **Twelfth Month:**____________________

(from Worksheet 48, Question 3)

Issue/Week One: ____________________
Issue/Week Two: ____________________
Issue/Week Three: ____________________
Issue/Week Four: ____________________

NOTES

MONTH 1

1. Ann Turnage, speaking at the first National Cancer Survivors' Day luncheon, as quoted in James W. Moore's *Attitude Is Your Paintbrush: It Colors Every Situation* (Nashville, TN: Dimensions for Living, 1998).
2. From Library Leadership 2000 Institute lecture, Schreiber Shannon Associates, 1998.
3. Annie Dillard, *The Writing Life,* as quoted in *New Day Revolution: How to Save the World in 24 Hours,* by Sam Davidson and Stephen Moseley (Brentwood, TN: Xyzzy, 2007).
4. Adapted from Daniel Goldman's EQ Model, as presented by Kim Langley, president, LifeBalance Enterprises, Inc.
5. Stephen D. Wood, "Providing Quality Information Service," memo, Cleveland Heights–University Heights Public Library, Cleveland Heights, Ohio, 2005.
6. Robert Fulghum, *All I Really Need to Know I Learned in Kindergarten* (New York: Ballantine Books, 2004).

MONTH 2

1. Adapted from Donna W. Howell, "The Politics of Library Boards," *Rural Libraries Journal,* September 2004.
2. Adapted from Paula Butterfield, "Creating a Resilient Organization," lecture, Butterfield + Laning, LLC, 2005.
3. Peter Smith, "Shared Leadership: New Ways of Leading," Peter Smith Associates, 2005, www.opi-inc.com/shared_leadership.htm.
4. From "Ten Behaviors of Managers Who Excel," lecture, HSC Workshops, 2009.

MONTH 3

1. Jim Collins, *Good to Great and the Social Sectors: Why Business Thinking Is Not the Answer* (Boulder, CO: HarperCollins, 2005). 12. Ibid.
2. Ibid.
3. Ibid.

4. Ibid.
5. Teresa M. McAleavy, "Look beyond Experience When Filling a Position," *Plain Dealer,* July 30, 2007.
6. Richard E. Rubin, *Human Resources Management in Libraries: Theory and Practice* (New York: Neal-Schuman, 1991).
7. Peter Carbonara, "Hire for Attitude, Train for Skill," FastCompany, 1996, www.fastcompany.com/magazine/04/hiring.html.
8. Adapted from Catherine Hakala-Ausperk, "Every Great Manager's Top 10 Tips for Excellent Performance Evaluations," presentation, 2004.
9. George Hutchinson, "Don't Just Survive—Thrive!" *Executive Focus,* March 2005, pp. 17–18.
10. Ibid.
11. Jack Ricchiuto, *Collaborative Creativity: Unleashing the Power of Shared Thinking* (Winchester VA: Oak Hill, 1996).
12. From Jack Ricchiuto, "Appreciative Leadership," lecture, 2005.

MONTH 4

1. Jon Emmons, "Management by Walking Around," 2006, www.lifeaftercoffee.com/2006/03/28/management-by-walking-around.
2. Cesar Millan, "The Dog Whisperer: What Your Pet Can Teach You," *Parade,* January 11, 2009, p. 10.
3. Library Leadership 2000 Institute lecture.
4. Ralph Daigh, *Maybe You Should Write a Book* (Englewood Cliffs, NJ: Prentice-Hall, 1977).
5. Eudora Welty, *One Writer's Beginnings* (Cambridge, MA: Harvard University Press, 1984).
6. John G. Miller, *QBQ! The Question behind the Question: What to Really Ask Yourself to Eliminate Blame, Complaining and Procrastination. Practicing Personal Accountability at Work and in Life* (New York: G. P. Putnam's Sons, 2004).
7. Ibid.

MONTH 5

1. Adapted from Joan Frye Williams and George Needham, "Update Your Service Mix: New Data, New Models, New Opportunities," presentation, 2008.
2. Adapted from William Schroer, "Customer Service or . . . Customer Servant? Delivering Excellent Customer Service without Giving Up or Giving In," presentation, 2009.
3. Williams and Needham, "Update Your Service Mix."
4. Steve Wishnack, "Customer Service at the Library: Making the Experience Meaningful and Memorable," 2006, www.lyponline.com/LLP_home/guides_art/Customer_Service_at_the_Library.aspx.
5. Ibid.
6. Ibid.
7. Williams and Needham, "Update Your Service Mix."
8. Paco Underhill, *Call of the Mall* (New York: Simon and Schuster, 2004).
9. Ibid.
10. Robert Spector and Patrick McCarthy, *The Nordstrom Way to Customer Service Excellence: A Handbook for Implementing Great Service in Your Organization* (Hoboken, NJ: John Wiley and Sons, 2005).
11. Adapted from Joan Frye Williams, "The Customer-Centered Library," presentation, 2007.
12. Ibid.
13. As quoted in William W. Sannwald. "Designing Libraries for Customers," *Library Administration and Management* 21, no. 3 (Summer 2007): 136.
14. Stephen Abram, "Reconstructing the Reference Team: 6 Ways to Sunday," *SirsiDynix OneSource* 2, no. 12 (December 5, 2006), www.imakenews.com/sirsi/e_article000703138.cfm?x=b8y6LvH,b2rpqjCp.
15. Ibid.
16. Barbara Pitney and Nancy Slote, "Going Mobile: The KCLS Roving Reference Model," *Public Libraries,* January–February 2007, p. 56.
17. Adapted from Andrew Sanderbeck, "Measuring Internal and External Customer Service: Utilize 3 Proven Steps to Increase Your Levels of Customer Service Satisfaction," presentation, 2006.
18. From Kordell Norton, "Catching the BUGG on Great Customer Service," presentation, April 2008.
19. Spector and McCarthy, *The Nordstrom Way.*

MONTH 6

1. Wikiquote, from *Wikipedia,* http://en.wikiquote.org/wiki/Yogi_Berra.
2. From Jeff De Cagna, "Strategy and Innovation for the 21st Century Library," presentation, 2004.
3. Peter Schwartz, *Inevitable Surprises: Thinking Ahead in a Time of Turbulence* (New York: Gotham/Penguin, 2003).
4. De Cagna, "Strategy and Innovation."
5. From Pat Wagner, "Hard Times/Smart Choices—Budget and Decisions," presentation, Northeast Ohio Regional Library System workshop, Cleveland Heights, Ohio, 2003.
6. From Becky Schreiber and John Shannon, "Where Mission Begins: Understanding the Organization," presentation, 2001.
7. Sandra Nelson, *The New Planning for Results: A Streamlined Approach* (Chicago: American Library Association, 2001).
8. Henry Mintzberg. "The Fall and Rise of Strategic Planning," *Harvard Business Review,* January–February 1994, p. 107.
9. Ibid., 108.
10. Jeff De Cagna, "Building the Strategic Association," *Forum,* September 2002.

11. Ibid.
12. Ethel Himmel and William James Wilson, *Planning for Results: A Public Library Transformation Process* (Chicago: American Library Association, 1997).
13. Adapted from Sandra Nelson, "The New Planning for Results: A Streamlined Process Designed for Your Library," Cleveland Area Metropolitan Library presentation, 2001.
14. Joseph R. Matthews, *Scorecards for Results: A Guide for Developing a Library Balanced Scorecard* (Westport, CT: Libraries Unlimited, 2008).
15. Nelson, *New Planning for Results.*
16. Chuck Hannabarger, Rich Buchman, and Peter Economy, *Balanced Scorecard Strategy for Dummies* (Hoboken, NJ: Wiley, 2007).
17. Sam Davidson and Stephen Moseley, *New Day Revolution: How to Save the World in 24 Hours* (Brentwood, TN: Xyzzy, 2007).

MONTH 7

1. Mary Y. Moore, *The Successful Library Trustee Handbook* (Chicago: American Library Association, 2005).
2. Ibid.
3. Adapted from "Ten Ways to Build Community Partnerships," *NEO Notes,* Northeast Ohio Regional Library System, Spring 2009.
4. American Library Association, "Library Advocacy," www.ala.org/ala/mgrps/divs/altaff/advocacy/index.cfm.
5. Marylaine Block, *The Thriving Library: Successful Strategies for Challenging Times* (Medford, NJ: Information Today, 2007).
6. Will Manley, *The Truth about Reference Librarians* (Jefferson, NC: McFarland, 1996).
7. Ibid.
8. Ibid.
9. Michael E. Casey and Laura C. Savastinuk, *Library 2.0: A Guide to Participatory Library Service* (Medford, NJ: Information Today, 2007).
10. Susan M. Heathfield, "The Five Teams Every Organization Needs," About.com: Human Resources, 2008, http://humanresources.about.com/od/involvementteams/a/five_teams.htm.
11. Kathleen de la Peña McCook, *Introduction to Public Librarianship* (New York: Neal-Schuman, 2004).
12. Moore, *Successful Library Trustee Handbook.*
13. McCook, *Introduction to Public Librarianship.*
14. From Becky Schreiber and John Shannon, "Relationship Power," presentation, Library Leadership 2000 Institute, 2000.
15. Peter Bregman, "A Good Way to Change a Corporate Culture," 2009, *Harvard Business Review,* http://blogs.harvardbusiness.org/bregman/2009/06/the-best-way-to-change-a-corpo.html.
16. From Cathy Monnin, "Corporate Culture," presentation, Northeast Ohio Regional Library System's Library Career Development Series, 2009.
17. Denise Reading, "Ask Dr. Reading: Creating a Culture of Innovation" *Cleveland Business Connects,* June 2009.
18. Ibid.

MONTH 8

1. Joan Giesecke and Beth McNeil, *Fundamentals of Library Supervision* (Chicago: American Library Association, 2005).
2. Adapted from Marti Peden, "25 Abilities That Matter," presentation (used with permission from The Hay Group), Surviving and Thriving in Turbulent Times workshop, Northeast Ohio Regional Library System, August 2009.
3. Peter F. Drucker, "Managing Oneself," *Harvard Business Review,* January 2005.
4. Ibid.
5. Adapted from Pat Wagner, "Why Everyone Has to Think like a Manager!" Pattern Research Inc., Cleveland Heights, Ohio, August 2008.
6. Deborah E., "Why?" in "Certified Public Library Administrator Program: Certification Process," www.ala-apa.org/certification/cplaprocess.html.
7. Susan H., "Why?" in "Certified Public Library Administrator Program: NEW! FAQ for Participants," www.ala-apa.org/certification/cplahistory.html.
8. Ohio Public Librarian Certification Program, "Ohio Public Librarian Certification: Overview," www.olc.org/pdf/LibCertification.pdf.
9. Camilla Alire, "ALA Announces Approval of Library Support Staff Certification (LSSC)," www.ala.org/ala/newspresscenter/news/pressreleases2009?jul.
10. Adapted from Kimberly Bolan and Zahra M. Baird, "Mentoring Matters: Pathways to Career Building," Kimberly Bolan and Associates, Indianapolis, IN.
11. Richard Leblanc, "Good Teaching: The Top Ten Requirements," originally published in "The Teaching Professor," October 1998, and reprinted in "Faculty Development: Teaching Tips Index 2009," http://honolulu.hawaii.edu/intranet/committees/FacDevCom/guidebk/teachtip/teachtip.htm#lessonplan.
12. Bolan and Baird, "Mentoring Matters."
13. Alan G. Robinson and Dean M. Schroeder, *Ideas Are Free: How the Idea Revolution Is Liberating People and Transforming Organizations* (San Francisco: Berrett-Koehler, 2004).

MONTH 9

1. Murray Dropkin and Bill LaTouche, *The Budget-Building Book for Non-Profits: A Step-by-Step Guide for Managers and Boards* (San Francisco: Jossey-Bass, 1998).

2. Public Agenda, *Long Overdue: A Fresh Look at Public and Leadership Attitudes about Libraries in the 21st Century,* 2006, www.publicagenda.org.
3. Ibid.
4. Dropkin and LaTouche, *Budget-Building Book.*
5. Ibid.
6. G. Edward Evans and Patricia Layzell Ward, *Beyond the Basics: The Management Guide for Library and Information Professionals* (New York: Neal-Schuman, 2003).
7. Paul R. Niven, *Balanced Scorecard Step-by-Step for Government and Nonprofit Agencies* (Hoboken, NJ: John Wiley and Sons, 2003).
8. Ibid.
9. Adapted from Deborah O'Connor, "Basic Budgeting," Northeast Ohio Regional Library System's "A Day for Branch Managers and Small Libraries," Twinsburg, Ohio, March 2009.
10. G. Edward Evans, "The In's and Out's of Library Budget Preparation," *The Bottom Line: Managing Library Finances* 14, no. 1 (2001): 23.
11. Adapted from "Requests Most Frequently Funded," www.greenfdn.org/frequently_funded.htm.
12. Evans and Ward, *Beyond the Basics.*
13. "Three Business Budgeting Mistakes and How You Can Avoid Them," morebusiness.com, May 18, 2009, www.morebusiness.com/budgeting-mistakes.

MONTH 10

1. Adapted from Kordell Norton, "Up and to the Right Leadership," presentation, Twinsburg, Ohio, 2009.
2. Jim Collins, *Good to Great: Why Some Companies Make the Leap . . . and Others Don't* (New York: HarperCollins, 2001).
3. Linda Patterson, "The Face of the Library," *Library Journal,* February 14, 2004, p. 43.
4. Adapted from Schreiber Shannon Associates, "Five Temptations of Managers," Cleveland Area Metropolitan Library System, "Skills Track: Management Style," South Euclid, Ohio, 2001.
5. Richard E. Rubin, *Human Resources Management in Libraries: Theory and Practice* (New York: Neal-Schuman, 1991).
6. "Cultivate Courage," *Communications Briefings* 28, no. 5 (March 2009), www.briefings.com.
7. Adapted from John McKee, "5 CEOs' Best Leadership Tips," *TechRepublic: A ZDNet Tech Community,* http://blogs.techrepublic.com/tech-manager/?p=447.
8. Adapted from Patrick J. Donadio, "Coaching for Superior Performance: Coaching Skills—The P.L.A.N.S. System."
9. Collins, *Good to Great.*
10. James M. Kouzes and Barry Z. Posner, "Leadership Is in the Eye of the Follower," in *The Pfeiffer Book of Successful Leadership Development Tools,* ed. Jack Gordon (San Francisco: John Wiley and Sons, 2003).
11. Adapted from Bill Grace, "Ethical Leadership," presentation, Cleveland Area Metropolitan Library System, Parma, Ohio, 2004.

MONTH 11

1. George Ambler, "Leadership Lessons from Geese," The Practice of Leadership, July 18, 2006, www.thepracticeofleadership.net/2006/07/18/leadership-lessons-from-geese/.
2. Adapted from Mimi Morris, "The Management Mix: Mentoring Librarians for the Realities of Management," American Library Association, Annual Conference, Chicago, July 12, 2009.
3. James M. Kouzes and Barry Z. Posner, "Leadership Is in the Eye of the Follower," in *The Pfeiffer Book of Successful Leadership Development Tools,* ed. Jack Gordon (San Francisco: John Wiley and Sons, 2003).
4. Kouzes and Posner, "Leadership Is in the Eye of the Follower."
5. Robinson and Schroeder, *Ideas Are Free.*
6. Regina Brett, "How to Make Tough Decisions," *Plain Dealer,* June 28, 2009.
7. Jim Collins, *Good to Great and the Social Sectors: Why Business Thinking Is Not the Answer* (Boulder, CO: HarperCollins, 2005).
8. Ibid.
9. Ibid.
10. Rick Ross, "Five Ways to Create Time: The Decision Styles List," in *The Dance of Change,* ed. Peter Senge (New York: Doubleday, 1999).
11. "Ethical Leadership" advertisement from Cleveland Area Metropolitan Library System, Parma, Ohio, 2004.
12. Notes from Bill Grace, "Ethical Leadership," workshop, Cleveland Area Metropolitan Library System, Parma, Ohio, 2004.
13. Jack Ricchiuto, *Collaborative Creativity: Unleashing the Power of Shared Thinking* (Winchester VA: Oak Hill, 1996).
14. De Cagna, "Strategy and Innovation."
15. Adapted from Stephen Abram, "32 Tips to Inspire Innovation for You and Your Library: Parts I and II," *SirsiDynix OneSource* 1, no. 1 (July 2005) and 1, no. 7 (September 2005). www.imakenews.com/sirsi/e_article000423643.cfm?x=b4TcM1g,b2rpmkgK,w. and www.imakenews.com/sirsi/e_article000436456.cfm?x=b5yKS7f,b2rpmkgK.
16. Adapted from Schreiber Shannon Associates, "The Difference between Management and Leadership," Cleveland Area Metropolitan Library System, "Skills Track: Management Style," South Euclid, Ohio, 2001.
17. Michael E. Casey and Laura C. Savastinuk, *Library 2.0: A Guide to Participatory Library Service* (Medford, NJ: Information Today, 2007).
18. Adapted from Lindsay Wittenberg, "Five Top Tips for Outstanding Leadership," Ezine Articles, http://

ezinearticles.com/?Five-Top-Tips-for-Outstanding-Leadership&id=661744.

19. Michael Moniz, "Top Ten Leadership Tips," Living Out Loud, August 2008, http://michael-moniz.com/top-ten-leadership-tips/.
20. Adapted from Aaron Kamanga, "10 Elements of Effective Leadership," Ezine Articles, http://ezinearticles.com/?10-Elements-Of-Effective-Leadership&id=879211.
21. Don Barlow, "Changing Service Models," presentation, Northeast Ohio Regional Library System, Medina, Ohio, 2009, www.slideshare.net/westervillelibrary/changing-service-models-updated.

MONTH 12

1. Adapted from Deborah A. Easton, "Empowering Your Staff to Make Decisions," presentation for Northeast Ohio Regional Library System, "A Day for Branch Managers," Twinsburg, Ohio, 2008.
2. Ibid.
3. Jack Ricchiuto, *Collaborative Creativity: Unleashing the Power of Shared Thinking* (Winchester VA: Oak Hill, 1996).
4. William F. Baker and Michael O'Malley, *Leading with Kindness: How Good People Consistently Get Superior Results* (New York: American Management Association, 2008).
5. Scott Sheperd, *Who's in Charge? Attacking the Stress Myth* (Highland City, FL: Rainbow Books, 2003).
6. Laurie Marotta, "Journal Yourself to Success!" *Library Worklife* 3, no. 5 (May 2006), www.ala-apa.org/newsletter/vol3no05/support.htm.
7. Catherine Hakala-Ausperk, "How to Journal Ideas," *Library Worklife* 3, no. 9 (September 2006), www.ala-apa.org/newsletter/vol3no09?.htm.
8. Michael Moncur, "Quotation #14197," The Quotations Page, www.quotationspage.com/quote/14197.html.
9. Leann Boyd, "If I Were in Charge: Fourteen Tips for Improving Management and Leadership," *Library Worklife* 4, no. 7 (July 2007), www.ala-apa.org/newsletter/vol4no07/hrpractice.html.
10. Sheperd, *Who's in Charge?*
11. Baker and O'Malley, *Leading with Kindness.*
12. Sheperd, *Who's in Charge?*
13. John G. Miller, *QBQ! The Question behind the Question: What to Really Ask Yourself to Eliminate Blame, Complaining and Procrastination. Practicing Personal Accountability at Work and in Life* (New York: G. P. Putnam's Sons, 2004).
14. Joan Giesecke, *Practical Strategies for Library Managers* (Chicago: American Library Association, 2001).
15. Jack Ricchiuto, "Breaking through Beyond Goals and Plans," 2009, www.designinglife.com/Jack/BeyondGoalsPlans.html.
16. Joseph R. Matthews, *Scorecards for Results: A Guide for Developing a Library Balanced Scorecard* (Westport, CT: Libraries Unlimited, 2008).
17. Cheryl Teresi, "Surviving Reorganization and Landing on Your Feet," *Library Worklife* 4, no. 10 (October 2007), www.ala-apa.org/newsletter/vol4no10/support.htm.
18. Ibid.
19. Marcus Buckingham, *The One Thing You Need to Know . . . about Great Managing, Great Leading, and Sustained Individual Success* (New York: Free Press, 2005).
20. Adapted from Marti Peden, "Attitude and Accountability!" Northeast Ohio Regional Library System's Library Career Development Series, 2009.
21. Kouzes and Posner, "Leadership Is in the Eye of the Follower."
22. Ibid.
23. G. Edward Evans and Patricia Layzell Ward, *Beyond the Basics: The Management Guide for Library and Information Professionals* (New York: Neal-Schuman, 2003).
24. Peden, "Attitude and Accountability."
25. "Erma Bombeck," *Wikipedia,* http://en.wikipedia.org/wiki/Erma_Bombeck.

BIBLIOGRAPHY

Abram, Stephen. "Reconstructing the Reference Team: 6 Ways to Sunday." *SirsiDynix OneSource* 2, no. 12 (December 5, 2006). www.imakenews.com/sirsi/e_article 000703138.cfm?x=b8y6LvH,b2rpqjCp.

Ambler, George. "Leadership Lessons from Geese." The Practice of Leadership, July 18, 2006. www.thepracticeofleadership.net/2006/07/18/leadership-lessons-from-geese.

Baker, William F., and Michael O'Malley. *Leading with Kindness: How Good People Consistently Get Superior Results.* New York: American Management Association, 2008.

Block, Marylaine. *The Thriving Library: Successful Strategies for Challenging Times.* Medford, NJ: Information Today, 2007.

Boyd, Leann. "If I Were in Charge! Fourteen Tips for Improving Management and Leadership." *Library Worklife* 4, no. 7 (July 2007). www.ala-apa.org/newsletter/vol4no07/hrpractice.html.

Buckingham, Marcus. *The One Thing You Need to Know . . . about Great Managing, Great Leading, and Sustained Individual Success.* New York: Free Press, 2005.

Butterfield, Paula. "Creating a Resilient Organization." Lecture. Butterfield + Laning, LLC, 2005.

Carbonara, Peter. "Hire for Attitude, Train for Skill." FastCompany. 1996. www.fastcompany.com/magazine/04/hiring.html.

Casey, Michael E., and Laura C. Savastinuk. *Library 2.0: A Guide to Participatory Library Service.* Medford, NJ: Information Today, 2007.

Collins, Jim. *Good to Great and the Social Sectors: Why Business Thinking Is Not the Answer.* Boulder, CO: HarperCollins, 2005.

———. *Good to Great: Why Some Companies Make the Leap . . . and Others Don't.* New York: HarperCollins, 2001.

Daigh, Ralph. *Maybe You Should Write a Book.* Englewood Cliffs, NJ: Prentice-Hall, 1977.

Davidson, Sam, and Stephen Moseley. *New Day Revolution: How to Save the World in 24 Hours.* Brentwood, TN: Xyzzy, 2007.

De Cagna, Jeff. "Building the Strategic Association." *Forum,* September 2002.

Dropkin, Murray, and Bill LaTouche. *The Budget-Building Book for Non-Profits: A Step-by-Step Guide for Managers and Boards.* San Francisco: Jossey-Bass, 1998.

Drucker, Peter F. "Managing Oneself." *Harvard Business Review,* January 2005.

Emmons, Jon. "Management by Walking Around." 2006. www.lifeaftercoffee.com/2006/03/28/management-by-walking-around.

Evans, G. Edward. "The In's and Out's of Library Budget Preparation." *The Bottom Line: Managing Library Finances* 14, no. 1 (2001): 23.

Evans, G. Edward, and Patricia Layzell Ward. *Beyond the Basics: The Management Guide for Library and Information Professionals.* New York: Neal-Schuman, 2003.

Fulghum, Robert. *All I Really Need to Know I Learned in Kindergarten.* New York: Ballantine Books, 2004.

Giesecke, Joan. *Practical Strategies for Library Managers.* Chicago: American Library Association, 2001.

Giesecke, Joan, and Beth McNeil. *Fundamentals of Library Supervision.* Chicago: American Library Association, 2005.

Gordon, Jack, ed. *The Pfeiffer Book of Successful Leadership Development Tools.* San Francisco: John Wiley and Sons, 2003.

Hakala-Ausperk, Catherine. "Every Great Manager's Top 10 Tips for Excellent Performance Evaluations." Presentation, 2004.

———. "How to Journal Ideas." *Library Worklife* 3, no. 9 (September 2006). www.ala-apa.org/newsletter/vol3no09.htm.

Hannabarger, Chuck, Rich Buchman, and Peter Economy. *Balanced Scorecard Strategy for Dummies.* Hoboken, NJ: Wiley, 2007.

Himmel, Ethel, and William James Wilson. *Planning for Results: A Public Library Transformation Process.* Chicago: American Library Association, 1997.

Howell, Donna W. "The Politics of Library Boards." *Rural Libraries Journal,* September 2004.

HSC Workshops. "Ten Behaviors of Managers Who Excel." 2009.

Hutchinson, George. "Don't Just Survive—Thrive!" *Executive Focus,* March 2005, pp. 17–18.

Kamanga, Aaron. "10 Elements of Effective Leadership." Ezine Articles. http://ezinearticles.com/?10-Elements-Of-Effective-Leadership&id=879211.

Langley, Kim. "20 Abilities That Matter According to Daniel Goldman's EQ Model." Lecture. LifeBalance Enterprises, Inc., 2000.

Manley, Will. *The Truth about Reference Librarians.* Jefferson, NC: McFarland, 1996.

Marotta, Laurie. "Journal Yourself to Success." *Library Worklife* 3, no. 5 (May 2006). www.ala-apa.org/newsletter/vol3no05/support.htm.

Matthews, Joseph R. *Scorecards for Results: A Guide for Developing a Library Balanced Scorecard.* Westport, CT: Libraries Unlimited, 2008.

McAleavy, Teresa M. "Look beyond Experience When Filling a Position." *Plain Dealer,* July 30, 2007.

McCook, Kathleen de la Peña. *Introduction to Public Librarianship.* New York: Neal-Schuman, 2004.

Millan, Cesar. "The Dog Whisperer: What Your Pet Can Teach You." *Parade,* January 11, 2009, p. 10.

Miller, John G. *QBQ! The Question behind the Question: What to Really Ask Yourself to Eliminate Blame, Complaining and Procrastination. Practicing Personal Accountability at Work and in Life.* New York: G. P. Putnam's Sons, 2004.

Mintzberg, Henry. "The Fall and Rise of Strategic Planning." *Harvard Business Review,* January–February 1994, p. 107.

Moore, James W. *Attitude Is Your Paintbrush: It Colors Every Situation.* Nashville, TN: Dimensions for Living, 1998.

Moore, Mary Y. *The Successful Library Trustee Handbook.* Chicago: American Library Association, 2005.

Nelson, Sandra. *The New Planning for Results: A Streamlined Approach.* Chicago: American Library Association, 2001.

Niven, Paul R. *Balanced Scorecard Step-by-Step for Government and Nonprofit Agencies.* Hoboken, NJ: John Wiley and Sons, 2003.

Patterson, Linda. "The Face of the Library." *Library Journal,* February 14, 2004, p. 43.

Pitney, Barbara, and Nancy Slote. "Going Mobile: The KCLS Roving Reference Model." *Public Libraries,* January–February 2007.

Public Agenda. *Long Overdue: A Fresh Look at Public and Leadership Attitudes about Libraries in the 21st Century.* 2006. www.publicagenda.org.

Reading, Denise. "Ask Dr. Reading: Creating a Culture of Innovation." *Cleveland Business Connects,* June 2009.

Ricchiuto, Jack. "Appreciative Leadership." Lecture, 2005.

———. "Breaking through Beyond Goals and Plans." 2009. www.designinglife.com/Jack/BeyondGoalsPlans.html.

———. *Collaborative Creativity: Unleashing the Power of Shared Thinking.* Winchester, VA: Oak Hill, 1996.

Robinson, Alan G., and Dean M. Schroeder. *Ideas Are Free: How the Idea Revolution Is Liberating People and Transforming Organizations.* San Francisco: Berrett-Koehler, 2004.

Rubin, Richard. *Human Resources Management in Libraries: Theory and Practice.* New York: Neal-Schuman, 1991.

Sannwald, William W. "Designing Libraries for Customers." *Library Administration and Management* 21, no. 3 (Summer 2007): 136.

Schreiber, Becky, and John Shannon. Library Leadership 2000 Institute lecture, 1998.

Schwartz, Peter. *Inevitable Surprises: Thinking Ahead in a Time of Turbulence.* New York: Gotham/Penguin, 2003.

Senge, Peter, ed. *The Dance of Change: The Challenges to Sustaining Momentum in Learning Organizations.* New York: Doubleday, 1999.

Sheperd, Scott. *Who's in Charge? Attacking the Stress Myth.* Highland City, FL: Rainbow Books, 2003.

Smith, Peter M. "Shared Leadership: New Ways of Leading." Peter Smith Associates, 2005. www.opi-inc.com/shared_leadership.htm.

Spector, Robert, and Patrick McCarthy. *The Nordstrom Way to Customer Service Excellence: A Handbook for Implementing Great Service in Your Organization.* Hoboken, NJ: John Wiley and Sons, 2005.

Teresi, Cheryl. “Surviving Reorganization and Landing on Your Feet.” *Library Worklife* 4, no. 10 (October 2007). www.ala-apa.org/newsletter/vol4no10/support.htm.

“Three Business Budgeting Mistakes and How You Can Avoid Them.” Morebusiness.com. May 18, 2009. www.morebusiness.com/budgeting-mistakes.

Underhill, Paco. *Call of the Mall.* New York: Simon and Schuster, 2004.

Welty, Eudora. *One Writer’s Beginnings.* Cambridge, MA: Harvard University Press, 1984.

Wishnack, Steve. “Customer Service at the Library: Making the Experience Meaningful and Memorable.” 2006. www.lyponline.com/LLP_home/guides_art/Customer_Service_at_the_Library.aspx.

Wittenberg, Lindsay. “Five Top Tips for Outstanding Leadership,” Ezine Articles. http://ezinearticles.com/?Five-Top-Tips-for-Outstanding-Leadership&id=661744.

Wood, Stephen D. “Providing Quality Information Service.” Memo. Cleveland Heights–University Heights Public Library, Cleveland Heights, Ohio, 2005.

INDEX

You may also be interested in

MENTORING IN THE LIBRARY: BUILDING FOR THE FUTURE

Marta K. Lee

Noted reference librarian and researcher Marta K. Lee offers librarians at all levels both her experience and her ideas about establishing a formal mentoring process at the library.

ISBN: 978-0-8389-3593-4 / 136 PGS / 6" × 9"

ORGANIZATIONAL STORYTELLING FOR LIBRARIANS: USING STORIES FOR EFFECTIVE LEADERSHIP

Kate Marek

Just as literature can be used for learning, the power of storytelling can be very effective when applied to leadership. Applying solid management principles to a library setting, Kate Marek provides the tools and explains the process of leading and managing through organizational storytelling.

ISBN: 978-0-8389-1079-5 / 120 PGS / 6" × 9"

MANAGING LIBRARY VOLUNTEERS, SECOND EDITION

Preston Driggers and Eileen Dumas

Quality volunteers can make a world of difference in today's library, and this hands-on guide gives you everything you need to maximize your library's services and build a bridge between your library and the community it serves.

ISBN: 978-0-8389-1064-1 / 323 PGS / 8.5" × 11"

LIBRARY SUPERVISION eCOURSE

Joan Giesecke and Beth McNeil

This self-paced tutorial is adapted from the ALA Editions book *Fundamentals of Library Supervision, Second Edition,* by Joan Giesecke and Beth McNeil. Whether you're a newcomer to the library or have been promoted from within, this eCourse addresses specific opportunities to sharpen your management style. Quizzes at the end of each lesson test your knowledge, while Further Reading suggestions point you to additional information.

ISBN: 978-0-8389-9076-6 / 3 HOURS / eCOURSE

Order today at alastore.ala.org or 866-746-7252!

ALA Store purchases fund advocacy, awareness, and accreditation programs for library professionals worldwide.